The Missionaries

Johann Baptist Krebs

The Missionaries

*The Path to the Teaching Profession
of Christianity*

Johann Baptist Krebs

translated by Kerry A Nitz

K A Nitz

AUCKLAND, NEW ZEALAND

Die Missionäre
oder der Weg zum Lehramte des Christenthums
published in German 1844
under the pseudonym J. B. Kerning

This translation into New Zealand English
Copyright © K A Nitz 2024

ISBN: 978-0-473-69440-1

Table of Contents

Translator's Note

For the English translation of Bible texts I have made use of the King James Version. Where I thought it would be helpful I have also inserted missing Biblical citations in the footnotes.

The occasionally somewhat idiosyncratic approach of the author to presenting dialogue has also been retained in parts.

With regards in particular to the eighth and ninth lessons, I would recommend adopting the stance of Dion Fortune from her *Cosmic Fortune*: "These images are not descriptive but symbolic, and are designed to train the mind, not to inform it".

I have concluded the translation with a summary of the author's life, taken from the obituary published by his Freemasons' lodge.

***

Introduction

Without exactly being a philosopher, that is, an academic who could exhibit a doctorate diploma, the word philosophy caused me in my youth some irritation in that I sought to form through my writing and my own contemplation a clear idea of it without, however, arriving at my goal. In this position I began to believe that this term was created arbitrarily in order to describe a few positive sciences in summary and to give those assiduously occupied with it a differentiating name. Philosophy, I often said to myself, means love of wisdom; a philosopher is therefore a lover of wisdom — but I found in the sciences which were assigned to philosophy none which could have given any particular enlightenment over the word wisdom. Hence I widened my judgement and said: the knowledge of all positive sciences is wisdom. On this basis I gave up for a long time the hope of becoming a philosopher, because I lacked the time, the means, and perhaps even the talent for learning everything in this class successfully — without, however, taking my eyes entirely off the matter and not feeling moved every time I heard talk of a philosopher of antiquity or of the modern era.

My father was a schoolmaster and thus biased for his profession in such a way that he knew nothing higher, and he fulfilled it with a punctuality and loyalty which, to the extent such virtues are rewarded, must make him all the more fortunate in the hereafter when he constantly had to worry and struggle in the here and now. Eight siblings sat with me at my parent's table, and there everybody can imagine that on a common schoolmaster's salary it must often have been wretched. But my father never let his courage fall. "God has helped before," he often said, "and will also continue to do so, and will care not only for me and your mother, but also for our children if I will no longer be." He often said the like, and strengthened us and himself by it, and truly, he was right, for we were never entirely lacking, and even before the departure of the parents most of the children were in part taken care of or so placed that you could look without fear for them into the future. My mother died one year before my father. He mourned her loss deeply according to all I heard about him, but bore it manly, and when he himself lay on his death bed, he said to the children present, "My trust in God has never disappointed me; keep this as an inheritance, and you will find it is the best capital which you can leave behind to honest children." — I was not there at his death. At the time I found myself in India and was thinking about philosophy and human destiny. But now I asked, was my father not a genuine philosopher? —

In order to instruct the reader in what way I came to be in that, in every respect remarkable, land, my earlier life history may be recalled here.

I reached in the house of my parents, or more correctly, in the schoolhouse of the parish in which we lived, an age of fourteen years and developed many talents for the position of my father, for which he educated me with all earnestness and zeal and sacrificed for me with paternal care many hours which would have been useful for his relaxation. He taught me Latin, Greek, geometry, geography, history, in short everything which is comprehended under the expressions of school and elementary knowledge. In order to equip me completely, he made the effort to enter me into a schoolteaching institute where one received, in the words of the director there, a philosophical instruction which made the entrants capable of teaching even the most limited natural dispositions the necessary elementary knowledge and of raising them into usable world citizens.

I made a very good start in this institution, so that I gave my parents much joy through the praise which was accorded to me. Out of consideration for my good behaviour I immediately received on my departure from the institution after three years a temporary position in which, however, I had to endure rigours, slights, and mortifications of all sorts and could thereby harden myself to bravely look forward to the more distant blows of fate which could meet me in my career. My parents knew nothing of this, and even if they sometimes caught a suspicion, I calmed such suspicions, since I did not want them to worry themselves for my sake. God will help, I thought in the manner of my father, and look there, the help came when I least suspected it.

Parson M. from Br. was travelling through our district in order to seek for the missionary institution in Br. healthy, bold young men who were well-educated in school subjects and not pampered by fate, and to have them taught at the cost of the institution religious instruction and the necessary languages. I reported to M., and found despite my awkward behaviour a favourable reception so that he himself undertook to effect an honourable dispensation from the consistory. My parents, especially my mother, were against my intentions to begin with; when I explained about the rigours which I had tolerated up to then, and contrasted it with the meritoriousness of my new profession, my father said, "The path you have chosen is rough; but God will help." My mother and I responded, "As God wishes."

After five years I was considered appropriately prepared and was discharged with five others from the institute. We were prescribed an itinerary, given tickets on a ship, and after we had seen a few of the most significant cities of France, even Paris, we arrived at Calais where after ten days we boarded a ship and saw Europe disappear from our view. As little joy as I had had in the part of the world which at sea I emotionally called my fatherland, I could not fend off an almost crushingly painful feeling when I saw the last traces of it vanish from my field of vision.

I and the five other missionaries who had left the institute with me grew intimately close to each other and burned to soon set our missionary zeal into practice. You did not hear us speak of anything but our high calling, but also not of the dangers which were connected with it. Everybody sought to strengthen, to instruct the others, and to shoo away the dismal clouds which sometimes threatened to rise in us.

I think back on those hours with emotion often. On dry land you seldom know what unity, brotherly love, and friendship are; but at sea where no change stimulates us, where the view into the future certainly shows us moral roses, but also earthly thorns in quantity, there hearts find themselves, there congratulations are not empty phrases, but rather outpourings of life which rise in their interaction to a power so that you would be in a position to leave this life for your friend and comrade without scruples.

Often a man of about forty five years of age joined our circle, who in deportment and education excelled above all others on the ship. He seemed to find joy in our enthusiasm, but he especially liked to take part in our theological discussions where he often made searching remarks, though they did not agree with our views. Most of us declared him to be a crank, even a rationalist, if not entirely an atheist. I myself, travelling to India not from the prompting of a fanatical zeal, but rather to make my temporary existence more bearable, judged his views from a different point of view. I thought him to be a man who in favourable life circumstances did not dedicate so much attentiveness to the theological principle as we had to do on account of our profession. I recalled on these occasions the tolerance of my father who often said, the confession of a good thing, without a good heart, is like a well formed tree which is, however, producing bad fruit. We could not deny him a good heart, since he often socialised with us while others were courting his presence. He seemed to be rich, for he was not only completely outfitted with everything which was required for a sea voyage, but expensively so. Often when others were regaling themselves with dancing and games, we were able to regale ourselves with food and drink, gather about him and take part at his cost in such discussions. This a few indeed wanted to refuse for the future as being against our calling, but he had won my heart; for I saw in him for the first time in my life a man who without ulterior motives wanted to cheer us up, refresh us, and even teach us.

Once, when we were sitting together without him and were expressing our views about him, I could not resist, despite my innate or inoculated timidity, taking his side loudly and in a way that made my friends astonished over me, and they declared that, to the extent I developed such oratorical talent in my career in the future, I would convert many thousands of heathens to Christianity. I replied that here it was not about the conversion of heathens, but rather of the false, uncharitable judgement of a man who over the entire voyage had treated us with obliging goodness, who, despite our limited means, socialised with us, met us amicably, and created for us by his interest also a more respectable position with the people of the ship. He had a good heart, and anyone who possesses that is a good Christian, and even if he had not yet been baptised.

This last phrase set off alarm bells in everybody. To be a Christian without baptism was for them as much a contradiction as wanting to turn midday into midnight. The discussion distanced itself from our designated patron and became a formal argument of biases where everyone gave his dogmatic erudition full rein in order to convince me of my error. I saw finally that I had departed too far from the sense of the word and was ready to perform a formal retraction when our man turned up. We were embarrassed by this unexpected appearance and did not know at all what to do. He saw our confusion, said quite amiably, "I seem to be disturbing here," and made as if to leave us again. I plucked up courage first and asked him to stay. He joined us, immediately beginning a conversation over a topic distant from our previous theme, and showed thereby a superiority of mind over our one-sidedness so that we all admired him and could not hide what a victory his conduct had won.

He did not tarry long, in that he explained he had only come to invite us that evening to a bowl of punch which he would like drink with us in remembrance of his daughter who had remained behind in Europe and whose birthday it was that day. My comrades murmured something about goodness and generosity, but I said to him the warmest thanks for his philanthropy in accepting such poor blighters as us in such a self-sacrificing way. He replied, "What I do is no sacrifice, but rather duty. You are headed for a career where at least a certain degree of dexterity and ability to judge character is necessary. You come from your schoolrooms where the world and humanity remain as foreign to you as the regions to which you are travelling. To the extent you would have had no other contact than with yourselves, you would have strode backwards rather than forwards in your views and in your behaviour in that one infects the others with one-sidedness. You are going to India in order to convert the so-called savages to Christianity. I resolved on boarding this ship to purify you of the dust of school and to turn you into free humans, that is, into true spreaders of Christianity. You marvel over my conduct, I see it; but the result will show me whether I will be in a position to lift you through my instruction to a freedom of spirit by means of which you will be able to have a more unerring effect on the hearts of the heathens than by sayings learnt by rote. This evening we will discuss this topic further and, so long as we find ourselves still at sea, debate it as thoroughly as possible."

He left. We did not know what had happened to us. It lasted a long while before someone said a word, and if I had not broken the silence, I believe we would have remained sitting silently until lunchtime.

***

The Missionaries

Since in the course of the instruction which we were awaiting, each one of us had to express himself in his individual peculiar way, it will be not be inexpedient to sketch of each one a small portrait and place them before the eyes of the reader in advance.

My story up to the indicated moment is contained above, thus only a few things about the development of my character in respect to world views and my dealings with others is to be caught up on.

In the house of my father I was accustomed to unconditional obedience, without apparent coercion, but rather out of love for my parents. In the schoolteaching institute I considered the established rules of the house to be sacred laws which seemed unthinkable for me to violate. But this love of order had, despite the good side of it, the disadvantage for me that I did not come into any contact with my superiors apart from the hours of instruction and thereby retained a timidity which did not allow me to look someone standing above me in the eye, much less address him. Diligence, obedience, and order were the principles of my life and gave me in respect to my studies a preeminence over the others which obtained me some distinction, on the other hand making me almost unsuitable for social interaction and the world.

In the house of my headmaster, to whom I was assigned as temporary teacher when I left the institute, no prospect was to be found for the acquisition of a freer conduct at all, to the contrary my earlier timidity turned into an unsociable anxiety. Only the love for my parents kept me upright at the time in that the thought of religiously being silent before them over my unpleasant circumstances conferred a peculiar moral strength on me. Notwithstanding this, I often wanted to sink into the ground; for hearing yourself constantly rebuked, never finding acceptance, is a state which you should not wish on your worst enemy. I will skip over the details of the troubles undergone and say merely that in the house of a bad marriage, badly raised children, and a ruinous household all the evils which are most unbearable to man turned up. I became as a result despondent so that I finally blindly gave in to my fate and did not believe anything but that I was chosen to taste nothing but unpleasantness. I do not comprehend yet from where I took the courage to report to a missionary institution, or why I did not despair in not repelling people at once. God will help, my father said, and truly, he did help!

In the missionary institution it did not go well for me. The teachers had liked me, and even if they sometimes objected to my unhelpfulness and timidity, they thought my knowledge would help me through in any embarrassments and lend me the appropriate courage. Whether this would have happened, if fate had not cared furthermore and almost in an extraordinary way for me, I do not know; I must say only so much, that the heavens could not guide me better than as it happened, in that I arrived on the entangled paths of my life to truths which went far above my expectations.

I had gotten to know my current comrades indeed already in the institution, but without coming into closer contact with them. I drew back everywhere, and so it happened that I remained without friends and company. Only on the ship did the crust of my human timidity burst open, and I connected in the most infinite way with my comrades in fate.

Grollmann, who in the institution, on account of his zeal, was only ever called Petrus, had been the son of a rich iron trader and ought to have studied in order to become an educated gentleman in the spiritual or temporal classes. But his father lost through misfortune his entire means, and thus nothing remained to the son on his half complete career track but to report to the missionary institution. He was obviously the bravest of us, and if the feeling of poverty which he had not known in his youth had not lamed his spirits sometimes, he would have been an effective leader for us, but he swayed back and forth between strength and weakness and could seldom find a steady point.

Reineck, raised by his mother, the widow of a good public servant, with a small guest house in the countryside, had inherited from her a certain character of civic behaviour, only the constant commerce first with farmers' children and afterwards with grown-ups in the country gave his conduct a peculiar tincture by which he himself and others were often embarrassed. A village schoolmaster, a knowledgeable man, but entirely unfamiliar with the world, had given him instruction in the elementary subjects and educated him so far as to make him suitable for entry to the missionary institution. His mother had died beforehand, and the memory of her remained sacred to him as long as he lived.

Bentheim, a good, pious soul who from the emotion of faith drew the courage to travel to India and become a converter of heathens, was the friendliest, most courteous of all, and always ready to be obliging and helpful. His father, a silversmith, wanted to have him study, but died too early; hence nothing remained for the son but to dedicate what he had learnt up to then to the service of Christianity and to become a missionary.

Sigmann, unconditionally the most knowledgeable among us, but in respect to thinking and speaking freely so anxious and limited that he could not bring forth ten words without stuttering and grimacing. The most infallible truths which a child almost knew to appreciate had for him full worth only when he could prove them with evidence from the writings of famous authors or from history. For this reason he was a positively academic and historical journal which was of use to us in many a respect. But this did not hinder us from making him the butt of our jokes and asking whether he then could even sleep without be taught about it by external authorities, by books and stories. He understood the valid remarks we made, but could not abandon the way once accepted. His father, an innkeeper who had not wanted him to grow up in the inn, had given him a schoolmaster to educate him who committed the mistake of letting nothing happen to his charge which was not proven by other authorities. His father died, the inn was sold, and since the estate turned out to be smaller than had been expected, he went into the missionary institution in order to expand his knowledge there and dedicate himself to the service of religion.

Lehnert, without exactly distinguishing himself in any way, knew easiest of all how to find his way in everything. He was the son of a schoolmaster and was mainly educated by his mother who used him for all sorts of domestic concerns, whereby he, though in a limited sense, obtained a sort of versatility by means of which he knew how to easily fall into line with the moods and views of others. With respect to diversity, his knowledge was more comprehensive than ours, in respect to thoroughness, however, he confessed himself that he came last.

This is the gallery which I felt forced to draw up, in so far as an utterance or a judgement is always more interesting when we also know from whom it emanated.

To this gallery should indeed be added, even if not a full portrait, at least a sketched drawing of the teacher; only, since we will learn to recognise him in the following in the entire fullness of his sublime way of thinking, I will not undertake to draft a picture of him which in any case would have to remain far distant from the reality. Overall I carry the conviction in myself that only a wise man can draw the image of a wise man. On the ship he was only called Mr Rückmann. The reader will get to know him more closely, however, and in him the ideal of a true philosopher was to be seen to whom the love of truth imparted the highest wisdom and provided a mirror in which he recognised God and nature in their immutable laws. The teachings which he provided us are so new and surprising that I hardly comprehend even now how one can have the courage to think them, much less to express them; they are, however, based so deeply and essentially in nature that every suggestion, even those seeming so incomprehensible to begin with, stood the test through practice and meditation in the most convincing way. But you will hear from him yourself.

***

First Lesson: Walking and Standing

Evening arrived. We went to the cabin of Mr Rückmann. The preparations to host us had already been made, and a well-dressed servant was busy, after we had sat, with setting everything on the table after a proper interval. The meal was not of many kinds, but tasty. Our host had it in his power to remove any awkwardness, and so we abandoned ourselves undisturbed to a banquet in which most of us had never participated in our lives before. To start we drank wine. After the greatest part had been consumed, the steaming punch arrived, richly surrounded with baking. The servant left and did not appear again. The host himself filled our glasses and drank in celebration of the birthday of his daughter. We supported him with joyful demeanours. He filled our glasses once more and drank: "To the prospering of our intention and to rich harvest after diligent sowing." After we had drunk for the second time, he began in the following way.

"I have made you familiar today already with my purpose of providing you with some instruction in respect to the profession you have undertaken, and will immediately get to work.

Anyone who wants to have an effect on others, be it on the educated or the uneducated, must first learn to walk and to stand. Your posture, your gestures and movements are indeed not bad, but still cramped so much by the forms of school discipline that no trace of that enterprising spirit which is apt for bringing a new teaching to foreign nations expresses itself either. You may possess in yourselves the necessary boldness for your intentions, but that does not suffice if it does not show in your demeanour and gestures. From the posture of the man we make conclusions as to his power; as soon as we do not see this, we accord him neither respect nor attention. You are arriving in regions where you will find no pulpits and altars, where no sexton places the Bible in the spot in front of you, no, where you will first have to reach the place to conquer it. How can you achieve that with the demeanour of a student which you still have, with the doubtful steps by which you move back and forth, with the wavering, mincing position which does not allow you to stand even for half a minute calmly before those who speak with you? What recommendations and support will an English governor in India surely give you if you are not able to approach him with steady stride and stand before him with firm steps? Confidence is the first condition for any important undertaking. Confidence, I say, but not brashness, must lead you from now on. Fearlessness, even if to start with only the appearance of it, must express itself in your actions, only then can you have some hope for success in your undertaking. The cited characteristics are not only necessary in commerce with Europeans, no, also with the native Indians. The bold, open posture finds admission everywhere; behind timidity you suspect a hypocrite or spy and drive him away without listening to him. From the gestures the dignity of your profession must show itself and the courage for it. From the gestures this courage itself enters our inner-being, and the previously despondent will, if he succeeds in it, become master of his posture, a hero whom no difficulty can ruffle anymore.

From what I have said you can yourself take away how important it is to learn to walk and to stand. Approach with confident steps, however, do not get far too close to those you have to speak to, but then, whether you or the other person is speaking, remain standing calmly! — Do not scratch your hair whilst talking, do not pluck at your beard, your clothes, or your fingers! Maintain your position once taken, and even if it costs you so much effort! — Try this amongst yourselves and by yourself, and you will in a short time feel a confidence of which you had no idea previously."

You can easily think what a strange impression such a lesson made on us. We had expected deep scientific revelations, new views over philosophical and theological systems, and instead received the directive of learning to walk and to stand. We were still sitting at the table, but did not know whether we should thank him, remain seated, or stand up. I, usually the stupidest, felt the unseemliness of our behaviour and forced myself to speak — "Our revered patron and benefactor has begun a lesson with us which in every respect seems to be that which is most necessary for us. Our previously limited way of life has constricted our natural life forces in such a way that we not only do not know how to walk and to stand, but not even how to give a sign of thanks. The son of nature, the countryman, speaks with highly educated men according to his peculiar way and seldom neglects a duty of thankfulness, but we, reckoning ourselves amongst the educated and the scholars, do not even know without honest consideration how to put things right properly. Our patron has seen this weakness of ours and resolved generously to free us of it. I accept his teaching and ask him to accept our helpless condition and make us into men in so far as our awkwardness and eccentricity allows it." — I also seized my glass in order to drink a toast, and did not notice that it was empty. Our patron saw it, quickly filled our glasses and summoned me to continue. But now I was unable to speak a word anymore. It was the first time that a stranger had obliged me to give thanks, the first time when I had expressed my feelings so loudly and without preparation; this worked together so much on my disposition that I could only hold back a stream of tears with the greatest effort. My comrades were likewise, even if not gripped to such a high degree, but without any of them having the courage to express themselves. Mr Rückmann saw our embarrassment and said, "It's okay! We must get to know each other better and make the attempt to display before each other the innermost stirrings of our souls. A man cannot accustom himself for long to acting without thought; he always thinks he must show us not how he is, but how he assumes that we would like to see him. This is a phoniness which we practise not only on others, but mainly on ourselves in that such a procedure passes into us and we lose sight of ourselves." — He took his glass, summoned us once more to drink, and continued, "To the celebration of this evening! May it bring the fruits which are to be expected from such young, hale dispositions yet to be spoilt by the world!" — He stood up. We got ready to leave, and made our bows as submissively and awkwardly as possible and arrived in our sleeping cabins in a mood which did

not allow us to speak even a single word over what we had
heard.

***

Results of the First Lesson

We sought out our hammocks, climbing into them so as
in our sleep to either dreamily repeat or calmly digest. I
could not sleep. After I had given my thanks to the creator for
the fortune of having sent us such a benefactor, I began thinking over the odd parts of the instruction I had received. Being
able to stand and walk, I told myself, is not an art though, for
children stand and walk. Certainly the walking and standing
of the child is still uncertain — with walking they sway to and
fro, but with standing they cannot find a secure point. We are,
however, not children anymore, I continued to meditate; we
are, even if still not completely men, on the way though to
performing a man's work. Learning to walk and stand! This
task has something of the disdainful about it so that in any
other position than ours it would have to provoke you to in-
dignation. He, our teacher, must be able to walk and stand,
otherwise he would not be permitted to undertake to make
such a thing the task of a lesson. Our teacher walks and
stands. Now one asks, does he walk and stand differently to
us? — Here I could not immediately give an answer. I asked
myself once more: does he walk and stand differently to us?
— Yes, my inner-being gave as an answer. In his gait the confidence of the man is expressed, who accordingly goes never
too quick and never too slow, always towards the goal which
he wants to reach, whilst we, like children, often do not dare
to move from the spot, then creep, spring, or sway, depending
on what our embarrassment allows. And when he is standing
before us in a noble, unforced, and natural pose then a man is
standing before us who distinguishes himself by his superiority as though he were a king and we his quick to learn slaves.
There is more behind this lesson than it seems at first, otherwise such a powerful difference could not reign between him
and us.

I first fell asleep towards morning, and when I awoke, my
friends were already occupied in various ways and seemed to

have forgotten the instruction they had received. I quickly climbed from my hammock, dressed myself, and went up onto the deck. The sun had indeed already long since risen, but a thin mist lay on the surface of the sea and reflected the broken rays in thousands of ways. The sun itself was at this moment gaining victory over the clouds and revealing a rare splendour. Nature is great, I thought — and man can watch and feel this greatness. Man can walk, stand, and watch! — But he can also only gape; then the watching is like the walk of an awkward schoolboy. For the first time in my life since I had become conscious of it, I raised my head and my neck as high as I could. I was startled by myself when I felt myself in this pose. Is man permitted to stand so proudly, so boldly, so certainly, I asked myself. Why not, I continued, in this pose I see the heavens, see God's omnipotence more than in the stooped pose and have at the same time the advantage of being able to direct my sight all around me. Man is built to stand upright and frees himself criminally of a part of the gifts of God when he stands stooped. I walked up and down a few times with firm strides on the deck and it seemed to me as if someone had taken me into training in order to learn to represent a king. I did not know whether I should rejoice or be ashamed. "The matter is too new for me," I said now out loud, "and hence my despondency; I must practise it, and then the results will come." I maintained my posture with doggedness, and strangely, the ship's captain, who was walking past me, and had not previously dignified me with a glance, looked me sharply in the eye and nodded a friendly good morning to me. As trivial as this circumstance may seem to the reader, for me it was decisive and effected in me a faith in our teacher which nothing would be in a position to shake anymore.

My friends came along by and by. The attentiveness which they gave to the weather and other occurrences delivered the proof of how little the previous day's lesson had occupied them. The discussion steered itself, however, to Mr Rückmann's lecture, over which the views were very divided. One person said, "Such a pose as he has is not to be obtained in inferior circumstances." Another continued, "Birth, wealth, and long habit must do everything here." I went into opposition and responded, "Every man must be able to obtain such a pose and such confidence if God and nature shall not be unjust. For me," I continued, "the scales have fallen from my eyes, and I have seen after having made just one attempt, one, that man was built by God for gazing upwards, whilst the beasts bear their heads horizontally with the earth. We are pointed to the heavens, not to the dust. We must look around ourselves, and that can only happen if the head moves erectly like a cylinder on the body. Hence, I solemnly declare, I have made the decision to follow the lesson I have received and also thereby distinguish myself visibly from animal natures."

My friends looked during this talk at me, usually so timid, as if at someone fallen from heaven. I noticed this mood, set myself erect anew, and kept both to the posture and to my claim that we had heaven to thank for guiding to us such a wonderful teacher. They disagreed, also making attempts, not with true earnest, to set themselves erect; only self-consciousness did not allow them to pay attention to themselves in that they always worried too much about the opinions and judgements of the others. I spoke once more and sought to explain that you could learn nothing in that way because you are only capable of feeling your posture through the putting aside of all other impressions. They did not disagree, only they thought it could not happen at once, but rather only by and by. I could not say anything relevant against it, only I did not like it, since I had obtained freedom from depending upon the judgements of others. "We are still students," I continued, "and no rational person can rebuke us if we do what the school prescribes. If I receive a new student for instructing in writing, I sit him straightaway according to the regulations at the desk, put the pencil in his hand and see to it sternly from that moment on that he remains in the prescribed pose. Thus it is here. The posture and attitude was given to us for life, and I am convinced that the more we proceed by the book, the quicker and more certainly we will complete the task." They called me a dreamer, laughed over my zeal, but promised to take the matter to heart and practise it according to circumstances.

Still more was spoken back and forth until new topics captivated our attention. Midday arrived, the afternoon crept past with the usual slowness on the ship, and finally the time had come to make our way to Mr Rückmann again.

***

Second Lesson:
Stimulants for Speaking

We had all gathered in order to follow Mr Rückmann's invitation, but the usual timidity held us back from approaching his cabin, and I believe we would have spent a long time yet in our indecisiveness if Mr Rückmann's servant had not come to tell us that his master had already been waiting for some time on us. We went with him into the cabin, but it occurred to none of us to apologise for the late arrival, or nobody had the courage, and if our patron had not spoken first, then I do not know how long the silent scene would have lasted.

Mr Rückmann seemed to feast for a few moments on our awkwardness, and finally said, "I was worried you might have forgotten my invitation, or did not want to hear my further instruction, and hence you will forgive me that I had you requested once more by my servant." We apologised with broken up expressions — "You are forgiven!" — "Your kindness!" — "We did not know" — etc., until he interrupted our murmurs and addressed us in the following way, "Be welcome and make do for today with a glass of wine which I ask you to drink in my company." He summoned us to take our seats, and we sat around a table on which a few bottles of wine and cold dishes were found. He put things right again soon by his uninhibitedness so that we allowed ourselves to enjoy the food and drink splendidly. After we had eaten, he asked how the previous day's lesson had agreed with us, and how had we slept on it? Each of my comrades seemed to want to say something, but since they had not made themselves appropriately familiar with the matter, they could not find any words. Finally I said, "Your instruction must be true, not only because you reinforce it through the noble and confident posture which gives you a conspicuous superiority over all the passengers on the ship, but because it stands the test at once. The entire night I meditated on it and in the morning immediately attempted its use. It may sound exaggerated if I say that I felt for the first time today my actual existence. Previously I walked and stood stooped and sunken into myself; I have raised myself up and had the experience that man must stand for himself upright and in a fixed position, if he shall not be the subservient vassal of another who has the courage to raise his head up. Hence I ask you in mine and my friends' names to gift us more of your kindness and give to us from your wealth of knowledge as much as you yourself believe that we can bear."

"Nice!", Mr Rückmann said, "You have begun well, and it pleases me to find in you an assistant for providing my instruction with safe entry amongst your friends. It is not about enriching you with my scientific knowledge, of which you possess enough, but of putting the means in your hands of being able to make it obvious and to serve the public good. Accordingly continue listening.

Man does not only have to walk and stand, but also be able *to speak*. Language is the highest characteristic of our nature and hence worth the effort of investigating and practising it in all its branches and applications. Being able to speak, it is indeed suggested, is easy, for all humans for whom the speech organs and the hearing are not defective speak. Quite right! Everything that lives, indeed even the lifeless, speaks, but not in the way the human is capable of speaking and obliged to speak. You have studied your grammar, know how to write a proper letter or essay, however, if you had to get involved in a discussion with a stranger who did not possess precisely your way of behaving or of speaking, then you would be incapable of expressing freely your thoughts and feelings. From where does that arise? Because your language is only a matter of memory which must be set into motion like a machine in order to hear only something of you, but your own views and feelings are locked so deeply in your inner-being that you do not even have the courage to call yourself to account over them. You will forgive me for allowing myself such remarks; only, in order to guide you with success I must show before your souls the step on which you are standing so that you learn to see the necessity of having to climb higher.

There are two sorts of subjects over which we have to speak in our life. The first are such as we have learnt from others or from books, which we carry with us on the slate of memory and read off on passing occasions. But this is then not actual speaking, but rather a re-chewing of that which we have learnt, heard, and experienced. In this category of speaking is to be numbered all that the greatest part of the educated, and uneducated, the greatest of the scholars, as well as the forest dweller speak. Even most preachers at the pulpit belong to this class because they have summed up artificially from the one times one of their science and drawn out the result for the sermon. This way of speaking, as infinitely much as it encloses within itself, is though only the water draining from a pond which does not still our thirst when we are truly thirsting for knowledge. The second sort of subject for our speech is of a different, higher nature. Here you dispense with the given and the learned, and consider only the needs of that which shall be spoken. Here experiences and sciences fall silent for us; here the voice of the spirit must teach us and tell us which words and phrases we have to use. Such a speech is the outflow of a lively spring for which the closer to the origin, the purer it gushes and like by magic the listener is notified of our feelings and thoughts. Such a speech, however, can only arise from the mood in which we find ourselves at the moment of speaking. This way of speaking is the sublime art in which the speaker, as though in league with spirits, develops all the powers residing in himself which are suited for the present circumstance, and informs the listener and himself.

If I am holding forth over the second way of speaking in a rambling way and with emphasis, then I ask you not to lose faith and to think that it can and must be used in all the affairs of life, should we not commit thousands of embarrassments. The instruction which I am resolved to impart to you moreover applies to speaking freely, to open recital, because in that the man can alone express himself completely and announce his independent worth. Only this way of speaking rests not on the material which our lecture treats, but rather on the mood in which we discuss our feelings and views. Anyone who feels placed in the mood of his material will easily find the right words and expressions; but someone who does not know how to attune themselves and mesh with the given mood will, with all cleverness and knowledge, not be in a position to hold a coherent lecture with appropriate emphasis. An example will make the matter easily understood.

When you appear before a friend, a patron, a superior, or in company, then you receive from the attitude, the demeanours, and the number present a specific impression by which your disposition is set in an appropriate mood. As soon as you are in a position to recognise this mood clearly, to direct yourself according to it, and to speak into it, it will help you overcome the difficulties of the forms of speech and give your speech a liveliness of which you previously had no idea. The matter seems certainly at first sight to be a puzzle; only, it is based in nature and hence to be safely tested through practice. We live for the moment; to be lord of the moment is our most important task, but we can only solve this if we are attuned to the moment and to the circumstances reigning in it and speak skilfully to this mood."

I had listened to this lecture with captivated attentiveness and felt tempted to test it straightaway. Hence when I thought that Mr Rückmann did not intend speaking further, I plucked up courage, raised chest and head up freely, though I remained seated, and began.

"The mood in which I feel placed is strange. Only, it is clear to me that to the extent I wanted to speak otherwise than in this mood, I would not find a single fitting word today, hence I want to speak as my heart feels, and straightaway make the attempt to the extent your teaching is fulfilled in me.

My heart tells me that you are a man like none I have seen before, and perhaps like there are none anymore. You have just spoken a lesson which seems to be as true as it is true that we must follow the pitch of the instrument in order to sing correctly. The circumstances, the surroundings are the instrument which gives us the note; when our hearing is sharp enough to meet this pitch, then by necessity our talk must make the natural impression; but if we are not in a position to direct ourselves according to this mood, then no learnedness, no scholasticism, in short no wisdom of the world can lead us to the desired result."

Mr Rückmann offered me his hand and said, "You have described the matter as clearly through your analogy as I could ever have been in a position to. The circumstances, the people, and the surroundings, indeed often lifeless things, give the tone. When we have the skilfulness to attune ourselves to this tone, or in this key, then the necessary harmony is present and all who hear our talk will be carried away by its force. But in order to put yourselves in the position to begin your practices without conspicuous cause, listen further: — Accustom yourselves to receiving the mood from all that you see and hear, and attuning yourselves to it and speaking to this mood. Watch early in the morning the rising and in the evening the setting of the sun, and give words to the impression received. Let your eyes sweep over the surface of the sea and look at how it unites with the heavens. Investigate the demeanours and the position of everyone with whom you speak. Look at the mast, how it boldly strives against the clouds. Dedicate your attention to every form, every colour, every material, and every motion, and you would have to possess very little feeling if you should not finally succeed in obtaining the mood for every aim in life." —

We were all surprised by the novelty and yet at the same time by the simplicity of what we had heard. Over the application itself doubt still seemed to reign amongst my friends, and Grollmann allowed himself the question, "Whether you then must not also think of words and phrases which are fitting for the mood? For it is though necessary that words and expressions agree with the mood we have received." Mr Rückmann replied, "You are right. Words, phrases, emotional state, and surroundings must agree with one another if the appropriate effect shall follow. Here we have come to the knot which must be untied should we learn to grasp the matter. The surroundings are the instrument, our disposition the ear to sense the mood, and the talk and its embellishment are the music performed. If I now wanted to claim that such a person as was not in command of their speech would find the fitting words for the talk, then this would be like wanting to make an impossibility possible; but educated people, and people of your standing to whom the study of language is day-to-day business may without timidity abandon themselves to the mood received and begin to speak without worrying which words and expressions they should choose. Here nothing is required but courage and firm trust in a power which is alive and constantly at work in us, which enjoys finding an opportunity to be permitted to express itself without the bridle of school."

We all felt the conciseness of this lecture and gave the warmest thanks for it. Mr Rückmann responded that we would only be in a position to appropriately evaluate what we had heard when we could resolve to make an attempt at it. We promised this and became involved by and by in a discourse on various subjects which did not directly enter into our field, and acted in our questions and answers, because we no longer thought for long, instead following the present mood, so free and unforced that it seemed to us as if we had first learnt to speak that evening. When it was time to leave, however, the old embarrassment returned to some extent because we did not know how to balance the too much and the too little; only Mr Rückmann came to our help with his savoir faire, and so we left him with the sincerest wishes for a good night.

When we arrived on the deck, we remained for a few moments, as if we had arranged it, standing in a circle where each expressed with his own words his astonishment over what had been heard. Lehnert, who seldom entered deeply into a subject, said, "It is to me as if only today was my tongue released, for I have never heard us speak with such facility before. To the extent I am learning to bring myself to give my speech organs free rein, and to not always hinder them with the brakes of our Philistine-like consideration, I feel I could keep on speaking for the entire night, and am myself convinced better things would happen than when I previously investigated for a long time what and how I wanted to speak." We all gave him applause and affirmed solemnly to practise and use the lesson we had received.

***

Attempts as per the First Sort of Attunement

The next day we soon came together again on the deck and sought to bring to mind the lesson from the previous evening. Each of us expressed his views on it. Grollmann expressed himself in the following way.

"If the lesson which we heard yesterday contains truth in itself, then we possess a treasure which cannot be bought. To be attuned to a mood, to lend this mood the organs of speech and to gush in open talk is a matter which I do not yet comprehend, but will not be ashamed to dedicate the courage and diligence to convince myself factually of what I should think of it. In order to reinforce my words, I will straightaway make the first attempt. The surface of the sea lies before me, over this I will speak. When I ponder what I should say about it, then my head is so full of images that I end up in confusion about what I should say; but I will begin to speak straightaway without brooding for long, thus it will sound approximately like this.

The surface of the see stretches far out around us, even further than the sight reaches. It is a magnificent view without though affecting us pleasantly. The monotony which reigns in it is not suited to delighting us, irrespective of which, it expands our chests because the powerful circle which it forms around us draws us away from trivial ideas and gives us an image of eternity. The circle has without this already the characteristic that it starts nowhere and ends nowhere, and if we then still think entirely that despite the wide extent of our circle of view we do not see the bounds of the sea, then speaking over the surface of the sea is an activity which enlarges the circle of our life, even if only for the present, and places us in this way at a more general standpoint than can happen in a narrow circle of vision."

"Bravo!", we all cried out when the talker fell silent. But he said, "If you desire that I continue speaking, then I stand at your service. I need only set myself confidently, and raise my chest and head to view the sea which is joined together with the clouds to set my speech tools in motion, and you will have a continuation of my talk, easily better than if I could write it, and which spins away by itself for as long as you feel like listening to me."

We all were very delighted over this impromptu talk, but without have obtained a conviction over the power of the mood method. We desired still further tests, and Reineck offered to fulfil our wish. "Give me a task," he said. "Well," Lehnert replied, "speak about our present situation." "That won't work," countered Reineck, "because this cannot have a sensory influence on me." I replied, "Consider our embarrassed faces and you will have truly visible impressions enough." "I will try," he spoke and began.

"Our present situation is in every respect strange, for we see ourselves at once set to a spiritual activity of which sixteen hours ago we had no idea, but which seems to be of the sort that, to the extent it stands the test, we will have obtained a method which can be of incalculable worth for our careers. What an advantage must arise to the popular speaker from it when he need not ponder the countless cases which can happen to him, but can draw from the moment mood and material for his talk. Truly, my friends, a paternally guiding providence has given us in our teacher a light which can guide us on all the paths of life and make us into true converters of peoples. Considering from this side our present situation, it is of the sort that we can only thank the heavens to see ourselves here together in the most beautiful educational company."

Sigmann, who for utter worry about speaking quite well had never spoken two sentences without grimaces and without faltering, said with unusual pathos, "I am astonished over what I am seeing and hearing. My friends who have already often made fun of the stiffness of my speaking, let me also undertake an attempt. Give me a task! I will make an effort to follow the received mood." "That's right then," we all called out. "He shall speak," Lehnert said, "and if he does not stutter and does not grimace, then the matter is proven." "What should he speak about?"

Grollmann answered, "Over the tall mast of our ship." Without further ado, he began.

"The tall mast stands before us. If I wanted to describe the goal which should be achieved by it, then the talk would be easy, then I would say that it is present to stretch the sail on it in order to drive the ship by the wind. But this leads to objects of memory and would take me away from the peculiar mood. Hence I will say: — The tall mast that stands so gloriously and vertically before us and strives towards the clouds is an instructive image for humanity. The mast stands erect, erect stands the man. Only in erect posture can the mast fulfil its aim and offer the sail to the winds. Is it not also so with man? Only in erect posture is he in a position to turn his back to the storms of life and go towards the calm of land. I could paint this image for eternity, but abandon it to you to make use of it. But I must speak about how I admire still more than the posture the art and the structure by which this giant tree preserves itself in its pose. Truly, if the human mind had achieved nothing but this, then we would have to admire it as a gift of heaven which is in a position to make the seemingly impossible possible."

Here he fell silent with a countenance which seemed to clearly say that he was astonished over himself. "The test has been passed", he cried out finally, "and I would like to fall at the feet of our patron and teacher in order to express my thanks to him for the glorious gift which he has made us." We all were deeply captivated by the last attempt and decided to record the current day in our calendars as the most remarkable of our lives, indeed as our second birthday.

***

Third Lesson:
Tools of Attunement

In the evening at the proper hour we were all already gathered and made our way to Mr Rückmann. Grollmann, who was at our head, addressed him with the following words, "You will forgive us if we perhaps appear today all too punctual." He replied, "Your punctuality is a proof to me that you are happy with me, and I can rejoice over that." Bentheim said, "The moments in your company are so precious to us we would not want to blame ourselves for losing one." Everybody said a few obliging words. He seemed delighted to hear us speak so unaffectedly, summoned us to take our seats, and we sat down again about a table set with wine and cold dishes.

But before we began to eat, I turned with the following words to Mr Rückmann, "We regret that you are making expenses on our account. The ship's sustenance on which we are reliant tastes good to us, and even if it is not also exceptional, we must consider that it is necessary and fruitful by virtue of our profession's simplicity." Mr Rückmann responded, "the small expense which I am making does not embarrass me, and concerning the simplicity to which you have accustomed yourselves, you are without worry over that. In the first centuries of Christianity, princes abandoned the opulent life of the court in order to live as hermits in the wastes, and endured it as well as others who had grown up in poverty." — We allowed ourselves at this to enjoy the wine and food, and as soon as we were fed, he inquired over the presumed results of the precious day's lesson. We presented a report to him over our attempts, and after he had expressed his satisfaction over it, he continued in the following way.

"The objects and circumstances around us determine the disposition and make us skilful at speaking about them as well as about all things which are connected in some way with them. But this is not the only sort of mood for our talks. We can choose from the quantity of objects present a single one and be attuned by it. For example, of all the objects which are to be found here in my cabin, I can have the tone of the speech defined by a chair, by the table, by a painting or another thing, and speak to it. Indeed, still more, I take a fork, a spoon, a glass, etc. in the hand, and if I am capable of feeling the form and material of what is held in my hand, then I have a mood in which I can speak about any task given me according to the measure of the mood." — "How is that?", Grollmann asked. The teacher continued, "I know that this way of attuning yourself is difficult to comprehend in that it borders on the unbelievable, almost on the miraculous, and yet it is thus grounded in nature and has been used at all times with such success that only those who have no feeling, no heart at all, can rebel against it. The first converters of heathens had neither book nor texts for their lectures; a rosary or a small cross of hard wood, ivory, or iron served them as a means of attunement and gave them the ability to have an effect on both the educated and the uncouth listeners, often as though with magical powers." Bentheim responded to this, "the cross is the symbol of the Christian religion. At the sight of it we are reminded instinctively of the sufferings of its founder, of his crucifixion, death, and resurrection." — "Quite right," Mr Rückmann replied; "but in addition we, those who have grown up in the Christian teachings, need no reminder, for that a little scrap of paper, a book, the names of our parents and godparents, indeed, our own Christian names would already suffice. The story of Jesus is written into our memory in such a way that we need no reminder to speak about it, in that one word, one feeling already suffices to lead that remarkable epoch before our souls." Bentheim asked for permission to make one more remark and said, "The form of the cross contained for the earlier converters of heathens a special magical power which originated from the sanctity of the one who died on the cross, with which it performed not only miracle-like, but also miraculous things."

Mr Rückmann answered hereupon, "You have touched on a point whose deciphering I would have liked to have left to your own free judgement; but, since the talk is of it now, I will attempt to give an explanation over it, as far as it is prudent to.

The first Christians ascribed to the form of the cross a special power tallying with the crucified Christ, whereby it was thought to work miracles. It is a miracle when the laws of nature are rescinded and the arbitrariness of an extraordinary power gets in the way of time and completes an action which lies outside the lawful plans of nature. But since this never happens, never can happen, we must limit the effectiveness of the cross to the named mood and set it in comparison with the power of other forms.

Every form shines upon us and attunes us to its peculiarity. The purer this form is, the more purely it attunes us. Anyone who is attuned through a straight line, a triangle, rectangle, pentagon, or hexagon, or by some other regular form, will be incapable of saying anything opposed to the truth. The earlier philosophers ascribed to the point in a circle the greatest efficacy. To others the sign of Mercurius was the most excellent of means for attunement in that it can be used both as a whole and in parts because of its composition. Indeed, you will give my talk no mystical, alchemistic, or hypocritical interpretation when I say to you that the signs of the planets served mainly as means of attunement. But whilst their descendants did not comprehend the matter anymore, declaring those wise men to be necromancers, makers of gold, and madmen, the matter remains though at its full value and, for those who know how to use it, it puts the means in their hands which the hypocrites, the judgemental, and the narrow-minded rationalists are not in a position to grasp and to use. The said forms are seen as the base types, the way you put forward with arithmetic the decimal system, whose laws work extremely simply, but produce results which are not to be counted and not to be measured, to the extent that every form, every colour, every material expresses an innate efficacy and can be modified and increased by any admixture."

Here he fell silent. It was to us as if we had been shifted by a sudden magic to other worlds, so strange did what was said sound to us. Warned from youth onwards about such views being the darkest superstition, we saw the matter was being derived from the laws of nature which, to the extent they were confirmed, stood there as surely and incontrovertibly as the laws of the musical scales and the relationships of numbers.

Mr Rückmann saw our surprise and continued, "What I have said certainly seems in our unphilosophical philosophical times unbelievable, almost miraculous; but for anyone who has the courage to make an attempt, it becomes as clear as the attractive force of the magnet, the warmth of the fire, the elasticity of the air, the electricity of the light, and the reflection of the person gazing into the mirror. Demonstration can prove nothing here, but experience everything."

None of us made any reply to this. The discussion turned away thence from the topics of the lesson, turned around incidental things, and we departed at the proper time, each occupied with his own ideas over what he had heard.

***

Results from the Tools of Attunement

The next day when we had assembled on the deck, the talk turned to the previous evening. Nobody wanted to cough up their opinion. Now I began, "We heard things yesterday before which we stand like frightened children and do not have the courage to look at them more closely. The first lesson led us to a conviction where no doubt remained anymore. The source which previously gave us pure water will not have clouded so quickly as to offer us all of a sudden undrinkable water. Experience alone can prove, our teacher said. Well, we will make attempts and then pronounce judgement." Grollmann replied, "How do we make attempts here?" I said, "Exactly as he taught. We plan to speak over this or that object, allows ourselves to be touched by a tool which we see or hold in the hand, attune our mood and begin the talk." Everyone cried out, "Well, then make the attempt." I responded, "Give me an instrument and a task." Lehnert left to fetch an instrument, returned quickly, and said, "Here is a pair of pliers! Speak over the duties of men." I took the pliers in my right hand, looked at the two cutting jaws with which one cut nails, and it was no different than as if I were feeling the sharpness of them in my inner-being. I also thought I could feel in myself the pin which held together the two pieces where they crossed. When I had prepared myself for about a minute in this way, I began.

"I shall speak about the duties of men! They are strict and imperative. Much indeed excuses itself when you do not know the extent of your duties. But directly this is the greatest breach of duty, to the extent everybody in the sphere of impact allocated to them knows their duties and would not have otherwise acceded to them. We, for example, have made it our duty to travel to foreign lands and obtain adherents for Christianity. Now I ask, are we carrying out our duty surely to this end? When I assess the matter as it is, I must answer: no! For what have we done for our calling of our own accord? Answer: nothing! Had not a benefactor taken us into training in order to civilise us a little, we would be extremely unprepared to go to India in order to convert people before whom we, in moral terms, would have nothing to offer. To bring them the Christian faith is certainly a good thing; but what merit do we have from this faith which we blindlessly inherit, and whose necessity we do not recognise through our own conviction, but rather only through commandments. The duties of men are given by God and nature, and must be fulfilled to the extent that we do not want to take up arms against these two incorruptible judges." — "Stop," Grollmann called out, "give him another instrument, otherwise he will denounce us all to hell." — Lehnert left for a moment and returned with an iron ring which he was lent by a journeyman smith. I put down the pliers, took the ring, held the open circle at chest height before myself and continued.

"Iron is strong. A ring of iron does not break easily. Why do men not take such a thing for a model? The individual is weak, enclosed in a circle we are strong in that each can hold on to the others and, himself protected, can also protect others. The first duty of men is therefore love amongst one another, because in the exercise of this sacred duty the others are fulfilled by themselves. Firm trust, firm sticking together, and steadfast loyalty in the bonds of love and friendship should therefore be the endeavour of each who does not want to put themselves in danger of having lived in vain." — Everybody cried out bravo. Bentheim drew from his pocket a silver-plated cross which he had inherited from his mother, and said, "Let me make an attempt." — He held it before himself and began.

"Religion is the surest guide of humanity. Making it live in yourself therefore remains the highest duty of everyone. Man has been created for two worlds, for the sensory and the heavenly. To the extent he only lives for the first and fulfils in it all his duties, he has not yet done anything of substance. He must go over to the invisible hereafter and learn to subject himself to its eternal laws so that, whilst still living in the here and now, he prepares himself at the same time in his inner-being for a different existence of which the current one is only the beginning, only the time of sowing." — "Stop! That isn't right," Grollmann called out. "A different task must be given." At this Lehnert, who had the most acquaintances on the ship, hurried away and brought from the boatswain's wife, whose daughter produced flowers for sale in India, a small rose, so artfully made that you could consider it to be natural. "Who wants to speak?", he asked as he approached us. Reineck offered to, took the rose, and gave the following talk.

"Life is beautiful. It leads through a rose garden, and it would be dutyless not to pluck them. Nature is our mother — she gifts us joys. What would we say about a child who spurned the gifts of its mother? That is an unthankful child, everybody would certainly say. Joys which life offers us to enjoy are not only allowed, but commanded, because without them we would never learn to appreciate the value of human nature and the all-encompassing love of the creator. Anyone who does not use a gift, even tosses it away contemptuously, sins not only against the giver, but also against themselves in that they take away the opportunity for their heart to become receptive to thankfulness and to become susceptible to pure love. Hence, my friends, I consider it my duty to say to you that we would be doing a great wrong if we wanted to close our inner-beings off to joy. No class and no profession is excluded from it, to the contrary, it helps in the most important affairs. For we may believe though that a friendly joyful behaviour finds greater reception amongst men than the pedantic advertisement of serious and cold legal forms. Men who rejoice with us will open their ears and hearts willingly to us and will take up the teachings which we are resolved to bring them all the more willingly when they convince themselves that they are not becoming poorer in joys, but richer."

We were all delighted over this talk and accorded him our unfeigned applause. Sigmann took the floor and said, "Be it associations of ideas, be it the effect of the object held, the results are so important that I feel like I have been placed in a magic circle where unknown powers reign and dictate the words. Only, provided it does not tire my friends, I ask for yet one more attempt. You know that I like to occupy myself in my hours of relaxation with geometric exercises, to which end I always carry around with me my etui in which the instruments for it are found." He drew it from his pocket, opened it, and continued, "Here is a little protractor, certainly a beautiful tool for determining the truth. Who wants to make the attempt?" Grollmann took the protractor, looked at it for a few moments and began to speak.

"Obeying laws is the first sign distinguishing men from beasts. The purer, more natural the laws are, the surer they lead men to their destiny. A right angle is the purest form of visible nature. Its image imprints itself on our inner-being and directs us unrelentingly to strive after the purest laws, to carry them out, and to become purely human as a result." — "That is enough," Sigmann said. "I admire with humility the miracle of human nature and have only the fear of whether I will ever be worthy of recognising it entirely." We were all moved and abandoned ourselves to our own thoughts until lunch.

***

Fourth Lesson: The Innate Tools of Attunement

Evening arrived. At the designated hour we made our way to Mr Rückmann. We dined as usual, and afterwards began the continuation of the instruction. Our teacher inquired, before he entered into a special lecture, over our views on what had already been heard and over any attempts which we had made. After we shared our news with him and he had expressed his satisfaction over it, he gave the following talk.

"The human is richly equipped with splendid gifts, but just as diverse are the means for drawing his qualities to light. We have treated two sorts of them, but the third exceeds those in a way that we often are required to look at ourselves with astonishment and say with the fullest conviction: the human is a true image of God.

We are all united over language being the most excellent characteristic of humanity, in that we are all permitted to designate knowledge and abilities as being in our complete possession only when we are in a position to account for them by means of language. To be able to explain about that which the human thinks, feels, wants, and undertakes therefore comprises the most essential part of his nature. We have spoken about two ways of awakening our language, the third we will discuss today.

The human can attune himself through things which he observes or touches, and speak in the character of the received mood about anything which others pose to him or which he himself and the circumstances of life pose. If he knows how to use his figure, then he is no longer in need of such foreign means though, in that he is capable of portraying by fingers, arms, and feet all the forms contained in nature. The outstretched index finger gives a different mood than the thumb, the little finger a different one to the two middle fingers. The flat hand has a different effect than the fist; with the arms we are capable of forming geometric figures; it is also a big difference whether we stand with the feet inwards, outwards, or parallel. The effect is different when we think of the heels and toes as the foundation of our position, or of the ankles, of the knees, of the hips, of the abdomen, the stomach, the chest, the back, the neck, or of the head in all its divisions. The heart, the lungs, the liver, the kidneys, the skin, the flesh, and the skeletal system bound in its angles and bends with the above are tools of attunement which contain a richness so that you would think nature would be exhausted by it, and bar no secrets anymore to humanity.

We can increase and mobilise the forms which we are capable of shaping by means of the hand still more through the touching of our bodies, can through the circumstances of position, the height and depth of each gradation of life's activity, strengthen, direct, and describe them, and transfer them to others. But this is an innate power which you should barely dare to speak about; meanwhile I consider it a duty to give you the necessary hints which can serve you as tips for your own exercise and set you in a position to completely obtain the thing.

But in order to put before your eyes irrefutably the law present in nature of being able to attune yourself in this way, I will bring your attention to three gestures which are frequently used in common life and bear within themselves the unmistakeable expression of our emotions. These are:

a) The outstretched fist.
b) The raised index finger.
c) The palms of the hands placed together with raised fingers.

Now should one find themselves in the situation of making a hefty rebuke of another, then he will, if he does this with the fist, need quite different words and expressions than if he only holds his finger up. If he wanted for the same behaviour to place his raised hands on one another, then the reproach would become a request. This is so incontrovertibly true that nobody can claim they are not forced with open healthy eyes in daylight to see it. We want to consider these three signs amongst the countless which we are capable of making as infallible types which deliver us the proof that, according to the character, expresses the content of the words in forms and signs, and through the latter the talk, the talk though is conditioned through the forms and signs. From this we draw the following infallible conclusion.

If the emotion expresses itself through forms and signs, then the character of the talk must be contained in the forms and signs.

As soon as we are now in a position to feel all signs and gestures which we are capable of making by means of the fingers, the hands, the arms, and the feet, the chin, the lips, the eyes, the back, in short, the entire body in height and depth, inside and outside, then we have obtained a source for our talks which is infallible and inexhaustible, and which, if we understand to use them appropriately, will give us in all the affairs of life ample supply."

You can easily think what a weird impression this talk must have made on us. Were the matter presented by the three named signs not so obvious to us, we would not have been able to give it any credence; but we had to give it a chance until we had tested the matter and found it proven by the performance. For me the three signs with the balled fist, the raised finger, and the hands placed together hovered constantly before my eyes, and I could almost not wait for the time to see myself alone and make the attempts. Grollmann said, "If every gesture expresses itself as unmistakeably as the three named, then it must already in advance declare the source from which it is then to be drawn to be inexhaustible." Rückmann responded, "Every sign, every gesture, every posture and position of the body carries its specific emotions and thoughts in itself; the entire art consists in learning to feel each one appropriately and distinctly, and to distinguish each from one another."

He engaged, in order to make the matter vivid to us, in various special discussions and even examples whereby the matter became so undeniable and clear to us that we thought to already possess it and be able to bring it into use. The time came to go, and we left Mr Rückmann in an unusually joyful mood and, when we found ourselves alone, made the signs with the fist, the index finger, or the hands placed together, and proceeded to bed with the promise of meeting on the deck punctually in the morning.

***

The Results of Attunement by Gestures

The next day we assembled in good time on the deck. We discussed to start with what we had heard the previous day; though nobody seemed to have the courage to get involved in a test, so I finally took the lead and said, "I see an indecisiveness has befallen us which does not agree at all with our zeal yesterday. So long as we knew how to attune ourselves with external means, we were brave, now we shall ourselves not have anything to do with it and are despondent and doubtful." Grollmann replied, "You are right! As enlightening for me as the matter also seemed yesterday as long as Mr Rückmann was speaking, I am finding no foothold at all when I contemplate it alone. Speak for yourself, what influence can it have on my way of talking whether I hold my hand in this way or that, whether I stand with my feet turned outwards or inwards, whether I stand straight or not. The three gestures on which he based his claim speak indeed for it, only cannot they also have won through habit such a power over us that they would have an influence on our talk and actions?"

I responded, "The reproaches which you make are not without cause. But even if it is that the habit exercises such a power, the matter loses nothing as a result, to the contrary, do we not obtain one more means for attuning ourselves to our purposes, to the extent that it then depends only on us to provide each sign through appropriate practice with the desired effect? Only this is as little the case as that a stooped posture should make the same impression as the upright one. The matter is confirmed too clearly through all the phenomena of life to even harbour the slightest doubt. The attunement through external tools has proven itself; now I ask why a form made with the hands, feet, arms, and body should not have the same, indeed even more striking effects. Here I hold up my index finger and thumb and summon you to give me a task." Reineck replied, "Speak about the influence of the forms on our ability to feel and think." I began immediately.

"You want to know what influence the forms exercise on our ability to feel and think? I say, in the forms lies the distinguishing signs of all species of being which are present in creation. From the form arises also the character of each thing, because it can only be felt and recognised in the way it is and portrays itself. Each animal exists through its form. The lamb cannot be a wolf on account of its figure, and the human would under no other form than the one bestowed on it possess such feelings, such insights, and such a unity with the spirit of the creator. Now if all powers are bound to specific forms and express their activity therein in both the vegetable and animal kingdoms, why should the same laws not also apply if such forms appear in another measure and other circumstances? — Straight and crooked lines and angles are the foundation of geometry and all that which appears to the eye. The mind perceive these relationships; the disposition, which is bound most intimately with the mind, must be able to be touched just as well by such relationships in that it exercises the same activity on the mind through the laws of beauty, propriety, morality, and of decency residing in it. But just as the mind is capable of dissecting the impressions of the disposition, so can the disposition deliver to the mind the material for observations. I mean, as soon as we consider this, the effect of our gestures on the mind and disposition cannot appear to us as a foreign expression of power, to the contrary, we would have to recognise it as a fault if it were not so." — Everybody rejoiced over this talk, not only on account of its content, but rather because they saw in it a proof for the power of attuning themselves through gestures. Each wanted now at first to make the attempt, and because nobody wanted to be inferior to the others, I made the suggestion that my neighbour to my right should continue and then so on until everyone in the entire circle had spoken. The suggestion was accepted, and Sigmann said, "I am forming a circle with my thumb and forefinger, and will speak attuned by this form over the effect of gestures on the mind and feeling.

The circle is the basic feature of creation, for all heavenly bodies appear or are round. They also follow the laws of the circular line in their movements. In the created being of the second degree, where the sun influences the earth, the laws of rotation appear to have stopped, only on closer inspection we find that, even when they permit themselves altogether a deviation from a matter, everything strives with the parts again towards the circular line. In the realm of life we do not find a single sharp angle; all transitions bend and wind both in bone, muscle, and nervous systems. With humans the circular form has, alongside the laws of the straight line, pointed in the feet, calves, thighs, in the bulge of the belly and the chest, and finally in the roundness of the skull, the crown of the human figure, to the most evident. Light exists. — It gathers in the centre of a circle, and in this way gives the circle and its centre a lively attunement to which we can speak about nothing else but the sublime and things reaching to eternity."

Here he fell silent. He seemed to think to himself for a few seconds more over what he had said, and exhorted his neighbour to now also make his contribution. The latter placed his hands crosswise over his chest and began.

"To the extent the received doctrine is confirmed, so the signs of prayer which we commonly see in historical images are nothing but such means of attunement in order to awake the spirit of the life in which we should pray. The sign in which I find myself is, I feel, quite suited to attuning our heart to piety and receiving spiritual impressions. It is an eternal life and an eternal love which not only flows through all of creation in general, but also through us as individual parts, from which we draw mercy upon mercy and as if under the eyes of a kindly guide penetrate safely and cheerfully through the floods of time." — He drew his hands away from his chest and said, "I think I have not done badly." We all gave him acknowledgement of our satisfaction and summoned his neighbour Reineck to make the attempt. He said, "I recall the image of Christ on a copper tablet, where he was explaining to his disciples the word, and I saw his right hand on his left breast, his thumb outwards, the other four fingers laid horizontally on each other. I will make my attempt in this pose and speak about it." He rose and stood as he had described, beginning thus.

"When you do not hear the prophets, you also do not hear the word; but anyone who receives the spirit of it will walk in their footsteps and become aware of the secrets of the word. It is a living witness of the word written in humanity which can awaken us to life and offer us the key to fathoming the truths of the text and obtain the state which puts us amongst the number of the saints." — He drew his hand back and fell silent. He made an expression as if he wanted to think about something he had heard, and said, "It seems to me as if I have said things inexplicable to me. I will have trouble recalling them again, only it is seen as a task which is worth the most earnest contemplation." We were all of the same opinion and summoned his neighbour Grollmann now to speak. He began, "In Egyptian pictures you often see figures which sit on a block and place the right hand on the right knee, or both hands on both knees. We will hear for once what this position teaches us.

It is certainly true, you would think, that creation must be easily comprehended because we see it and its phenomena daily. Only we always only consider the outer forms, also rarely beginning our inquiries below, at the foundation, in that we imagine the essence itself lies in the branches of the tree, or in external phenomena, and can lead us to knowledge. We all know from experience that such a way of inquiring does not lead to the goal, and yet we do not abstain from it, because we fear walking a new path and gathering new experiences which could be contrary to our prejudices. We must move forwards, and the clearest evidence of not progressing is obviously when we always remain in the old place. Not progressing and yet saying you mature is the most despicable thing which humans can encounter. Hence free your legs of the tethers with which they are bound, seek and inquire for as long as you can until you obtain the conviction of walking on the right path and having progressed." — Here he fell silent. Reineck said, "Our friend has expressed a truth in his talk which only a child or the wise can say, and this is: the clearest proof of not progressing is when you always remain in the old place. I consider that the greatest part of humanity may take this truth to heart; for despite all efforts to progress, you see them constantly, indeed sometimes clothed differently, in the same spot."

Grollmann said, "We have one more talk to hear. Our friend Lehnert will completely remove the cataract from our eyes." The latter responded, "Do not expect too much from me. We are prosecuting a matter before which I begin to be afraid. To the extent there are such simple means of awakening our gifts, our powers of cognition, in one word, our spirit, why was it not said before and not to all men? I fear the most enlightened of all times have had cause to keep such a doctrine hidden in order to not put into the wrong hands a tool for harming oneself and others." — This opening gave cause for a dispute in which everyone uttered their opinions, and whose result ended up being that no means for the obtaining of knowledge may be withdrawn from humanity without committing a theft against it. At this Lehnert folded both hands and began.

"It is certainly true that man is not as he should be. A perfection could be created in the world which would almost be heaven's equal; only this seems to be unable to be produced in the here and now, because we are at the mercy of too many temptations, flesh and blood also desire their due, and we can therefore only wish to complete this pilgrimage in such a way that, without taking from the creature its rights, we nevertheless obtain the upper hand for the heavenly light in us and make ourselves worthy of entry into the eternal home." — He fell silent. His face showed that gesture, words, and disposition must have been in complete agreement. We rejoiced at this talk and praised each other for dedicating the entire day to the experience of it. We parted in silence, each to his own business, and remained in this mood until we went to Mr Rückmann that evening.

***

Fifth Lesson: Attunement through Imagined Tools

After we had told our teacher what attempts we had made, and how they had turned out, he continued, after we had enjoyed some food, his instruction.

"We have dealt with three kinds of means for awakening the word or the talk in us. As splendid as the results from them may also be, eternal love did not stop there, but gave us the means to this end, means which elude visibility entirely and offer in their use the most complete freedom. It is not only the visible circumstances, tools, and gestures which possess the power of attuning us, no, already the *imagined* suffices for that. The imagined surface of the sea, the imagined mast, the imagined tools for attunement, and imagined gestures, as soon as we possess enough uninhibitedness to imagine them vividly, deliver for it often even more genuine results than the visible equivalents. Here is the fertile field which was known in all ages and denied in all ages. It is those means which enthused the poets, led them into the chambers of beauty and virtue and to the battlefield; which directed the chisel of the sculptor and gave the brush of the painter its lively magic; it finally led the faithful to the sanctum of God and held up before them the duties of a religious life. The power which showed the poet, the sculptor, the painter new regions, strange customs, and human natures placed far more exaltedly can also open the curtains for us to eternity and reveal images of an eternal life. To deny the flight to eternity and the means to get to know its laws means forgoing its dignity and confessing that you, like the ostrich, cannot think further than the eyes reach. I would desire to possess words enough to make really insistent for you this way of attuning yourself and to induce you thereby to an activity which frees one from the dust and can draw from purely intellectual products under all circumstances the sustenance of life."

This lecture, although in its content touching purely intellectual powers, did not make a strange impression on us like the earlier one, in that the intimations clung more to the views of the world and agreed with the usual concepts of powers of imagination, fantasy, psychology, and enthusiasm for art. Nevertheless we were very content because this activity, connected with the preceding ones, allowed an infinitely greater expansion and provided us at the same time with a freedom which knows no bounds and cannot be suppressed by any power on earth anymore. We used these views to pronounce to each other on it and to place our small bit of positive knowledge in the most advantageous light. Mr Rückmann seemed to fall in with us, for he aligned himself with our schoolmasterly tone and gave some good hints.

At the close he brought the conversation once more to the earlier lecture and said, "I consider it expedient to close with the theme with which we began the evening. It concerns forming ideas yourselves, with the help of memory, also of imagination, which can create new ideas and thereby work on our cognitive faculties, but principally on the liveliness of our language and its expression. To describe the intellectual activity in this area, years would not suffice; to the contrary, in the mythological images of all the nations which are frequently emerging in our time are to be found the most unmistakeable features of this intellectual effect, and which assessed only from this point of view allows a natural explanation in agreement with reason. I possess here a substantial collection of copperplate engravings which are all more or less aimed at our lesson. I will leave them in your care to use and ask you to dedicate your entire attention to the meaning of them." — He handed over to us a large portfolio with the aforementioned copperplate engravings, we found this time in fact no words to express our thanks appropriately, and left him with feelings of our deepest veneration.

***

The Trainees are Embarrassed

The next morning we gathered at the accustomed time. We looked at the engravings, but could not yet find any actual information. Sigmann said, "Such a thing you must look at very frequently. Now we are only seeing the forms; — the spirit of it can, like with all subjects, only be unveiled by time." Now we planned to make attempts by means of thought-up tools of attunement; only it was not working out successfully. I finally took the lead and said, "It seems to me we are lacking the appropriate uninhibitedness for the new manner of action. Already with the first means of attunement, although visible signs captivated our senses, it was something difficult to lay claim to, but here, where we are directed to our innermost, extrasensory powers, eyes and ears, fantasy and desires swarm in us and around us, and the imagined means of help vanish in the mist of these images. I am convinced that the imagined tools of attunement, provided we obtain the power of holding them firmly, must work as securely, indeed I would like to believe even far more purely than the first."

This claim seemed to be clear to everyone, and they made the effort to obtain the stipulated uninhibitedness. Grollmann finally cried out, "Stop! I have it! It is difficult to hold on to the tool, but I feel that it is possible. Certainly our body must also help in it; it must not waver and give way, if the imagined image is to not vanish again. I think of a pick hammer like the stonemasons use; it hovers before my soul and shall give me the mood. Over what should I speak?" "Over our profession", a few gave in answer. "Well, then listen!", he replied and began.

"The world desires a doctrine in order to imagine the hereafter. We are called to bring such a thing to the uncultured peoples. But what doctrine do we want to bring them? Is it also the best which you can give? I have already often thought about the sole salvation of which every religion boasts and found doubt instead of conviction. If we come to the peoples who venerate God perhaps under a different name and under different outward forms just as intimately as we do, will it then belong to our profession to force our doctrine on them? The mood which now reigns in me says with the apostle Paul that God did not let any people go unwitnessed*, and brings me to the question of whether we are authorised to rebuke

---

*   [Tr.: cf. Romans 2:11.]

such a testimony and assert ours alone? — I am getting confused again and suggest we ask our teacher to give us instruction over this." — Here he made a motion with his hand away from his chest and looked as if he were awakening from a dream. We all felt strangely stirred over the raised doubt, and Sigmann, instead of waiting until evening, made the suggestion that someone should attune themselves through the imagined form of the cross and give us further discussion on this topic.

Bentheim decided to do it, and once he believed he was in the mood, he said, "The Christian religion is a summary of all the divine doctrines which we meet in the history of the world. It is a perfect whole in that it starts with the history of humanity and connects their confessors in this way with God. It has its cause in the needs of humanity, because the human can only be saved through the spirit of God and through the elimination of sin by death. No other religion speaks of such a salvation, and hence its propagation is the greatest benefaction. Every human, even the most perfect, has moments where he feels his weakness and sinfulness, and easily loses the faith in virtue and in himself. A religion which expresses salvation from sin and death so openly and purely is certainly a light which should illuminate all the people who are in this world." — Here he fell silent, and we all had to confess that what had been said was entirely suited, even if not to placate, to at least weaken our doubt.

We all made attempts one after another; but since these only delivered wavering results and lacked any free view, they will be passed over here. But everyone was agreed that uninhibitedness and secure posture were essential conditions and without such the means of attunement vanished from our imaginations and no longer exercised any influence.

***

Sixth Lesson: The Attunement by Words

We did not go to Mr Rückmann that evening as cheerfully as on the previous days. He sensed this, and after we had enjoyed some food, he began to speak.

"It seems my lesson yesterday has not born any fruits yet, because you are so subdued. I did not expect anything else, in that the task is difficult and desires a self-mastery of both the internal and external attitudes which you can only obtain through frequent practice. If uninhibitedness is already necessary for attuning yourself with the visible sorts, then here it must be present to a degree where no impressions from outside, no emotions, no ideas, no prejudices, no passions, in short no other impressions may affect us, should the imagined means of attunement not darken or even be entirely falsely felt.

Uninhibitedness, I say it once more, is the first condition for learning to feel the stirrings of our life. To come to an understanding over it, we want to not so much investigate what uninhibitedness is, as consider rather the hindrances which stand in its way.

The man should according to our task be master of his language and his speech. We have to this end named specific means of attunement which, however, in order to express their effectiveness must be distinctly felt. To a clear feeling for life belongs an unclouded state of the soul. Any self-consciousness clouds not only the soul, but rather hangs a veil over it so that it either does not see the objects at all, or in a false light. On this basis it is extremely necessary to set aside all hindrances which disturb our uninhibitedness, and to get to know them to this end.

The first hindrance here is the natural timidity of the man before a matter whose outcome he does not see. The free speaker, before he begins his talk, does not know how it will succeed and how it will end. Like the soldier who to break through a line ventures into the struggle uncertain of whether he will gain victory, so too does the free speaker undertake his talk supported by nothing but technical dexterity of language, bold courage to strike through all the hindrances of rhetorical constructions, and finally by the mood which he preserves by means of the seen, grasped, or imagined tools of attunement. — Everyone realises easily how much belongs to surviving as a hero on such a subtle battleground.

Another hindrance, just as large, are the preconceived opinions and prejudices which we labour under for the most part, where we can only with difficulty succeed in following the natural mood and speaking against our aged views. Anyone who in the cause of his talk runs into ideas which he thinks must not be expressed; anyone who sticks to views and seeks to weave such into his talk against the mood, they become entangled, despite boldness and dexterity, in self-made snares and will obtain no fruits for their efforts.

A massive hindrance to uninhibitedness furthermore is the addiction of people to getting mixed up in specialities and personalities which either offend or stimulate arrogance. Generality possesses a kingly power, as we already see in common life. Anyone who has made it a rule at every opportunity with any discourse to only have the matter in mind and subordinate special cases to the generality is always heard with pleasure, whereas those who worry about personalities only see the little marks when a dull-witted head is viewed, which you would in the best case look at with sympathy, if not with contempt.

The greatest hindrance to the maintaining of the necessary uninhibitedness consists of the intractability, awkwardness, and yet at the same time the inconstancy of our body which contributes so essentially to fixing our feelings and thoughts on a point.

The body is intractable because it has obtained too much dominance and likes far too much to show how it longs for whims, leisureliness, lethargy, and frequently also vanity and pride. — Here you can only with effort get it used to setting its posture in accord with our intention. — It is only to be dissuaded with difficulty from accustomed habits which often do not stand in the slightest accord with the feelings and ideas of the moment and hence work against the necessary mood. — The intractability of the body is increased still more by the limitedness of our views, as if the heart alone were able to feel stirrings of the soul. The soul does not reside in a single part, but rather in all the limbs and organs of the body, and must stir and feel in them, otherwise we exclude them from life and we relinquish its natural effect. Every part of our body is a natural means for attunement which, to the extent we know how to select it, provides us with an immense wealth. But the limbs and organs do not only work individually, no, the human can make himself capable of putting in action several, even all of them together in one mood and, like the organist with all the stops pulled out, work with irresistible force on his audience.

Awkwardness is in this respect, even when not innate, of an instilled character. — We have our favourite gestures, our favourite poses according to which the mood of the entire body is mostly directed, even if the circumstances and tools desire a different mood. When we succeed also in feeling the disharmony, the parts that have been held too long in inactivity do not want at all to resign themselves to mesh with the intended mood and cooperate appropriately. This affair can only be remedied by frequent practice in that it is here about learning to give the limbs and organs that direction which is suited to the intended effectiveness.

Just as obstructive as awkwardness is the inconstancy of the body. — The human enjoys change. — When he cannot obtain this in his life circumstances, he looks for it in changing his gestures and his bodily position. The most difficult thing for the child is to stand or to sit calmly. In the body in which the soul plays there reigns a constant stimulus towards mobility. Only, as we know from experience, no impression and no feeling is able to be judged in the commotion. The body has a keynote; all the parts must attune themselves with this, otherwise they not only exclude themselves, but also numb the natural mood. How necessary the harmonisation of all the parts is can be judged by anyone who is able to imagine how unusable an organ would have to be where no register agreed with the next. You learn the organ by educating the hearing, by educating your feelings you attune the body.

Firm and confident posture is necessary here because otherwise the natural and characteristic vibration is impeded and no specific emotion can be felt. In common life we see how difficult it must be to achieve some assuredness here. Often we slouch, and belly, chest, and stomach, often even the head lose their harmony. Often you spread yourself, throw head and chest back, and overrule the back in which the marrow of life flows. The feet mince to and fro, and you do not know anymore where the centre of balance is. The hands are sometimes above, sometimes below, and make us confused in such a way that we are no longer in a position to feel anything anymore. When we walk, the steps are often too quick, often too slow, often too short, or too long, and all this at the cost of natural harmony. The human must know his seven stages, the soul of his body in which the creator has placed all the power of thinking and feeling, otherwise he cannot say he knows himself. The figure of the human is the Jacob's ladder on which he shall climb up to heaven. — He that hath ears to hear, Christ said, let him hear*. — According to what has been said, this means whoever has the feeling to feel, let him feel; for in the realm of life the feeling represents eyes and ears and sees and hears at the same time in that it feels.

So much over the hindrances which interrupt the necessary uninhibitedness for awakening the inner-being and for attuning us for our talk, and which are often contrary to it. I had to discuss them at length because they are already suppressing some ability, or have already stifled some fruit from blossoming. But in order to not come to a standstill in the actual lesson, I will make you familiar with a means of attuning yourself which far exceeds the former ones in reliability and assuredness, in so far as, in that you think it, it must also be felt, and in that you feel it, it must also be thought. Here, if we go earnestly to work, no disturbance through any hindrance is possible because we must only want in order to put it to use. Listen! —

The means of attunement of which I now speak were at all times considered by many to be a mere fantasy and hence not believed, comprehended by a few and brought into practice

---

*   [Tr.: Matthew 11:15.]

by still fewer. On this basis I would also not have made you familiar with it, if you had not intended to travel to India where the same practice still reigns amongst the Brahmans, and of which those who intend to bring to those peoples a new spiritual doctrine must by necessity know it in order to not be attacked with unfamiliar weapons. This is the art of attuning yourself with words. Every Brahman who reaches a certain stage receives from the chief Brahman their own word which must serve them as means of attunement in all affairs of life, in talking, praying, in giving assistance and ideas of consolation for misfortune and illness. The first Christian church fathers made use of these means with the best results, and it depends only on learning to feel and think such a word in yourself, thus its effect is as certain and infallible as no other in all of creation."

Anybody who has been paying attention to what was said can imagine the mood in which we were put by this talk. Attuning yourself with words was so strange and new to us that we could not hold back our surprise and displeasure and begged Mr Rückmann insistently to give us more precise hints, to tell us a few such words, and to instruct us over their use. He responded with unusual earnestness, "I would like to comply with your bidding and provide a complete guide, but — I must not. I can only say so much as that we produce by means of this way of attunement a power in ourselves which raises our existence to a standpoint where we forget the fleetingness of time and associate ourselves already in the here and now with eternity."

Here he fell silent. — If our surprise and displeasure were great previously, these last remarks were not suited to diminishing it. As much as we begged him though to give us a more precise explanation, he kept to his remark, "I must not." — The time approached for us to take our leave, and we left Mr Rückmann that day no differently than as if we had been dreaming and would now like to come to an understanding in silence over the images of the dream. It was as if nobody could trust themselves to speak with the others so as to not destroy the impression received and forget the intimations.

***

New Embarrassment

I could not sleep. To be able to attune myself with words sounded so strange to me, as if it lay outside the realms of possibility. I still recalled my former doubt about attaching a positive effect to words or language, since it is the exclusive feature of our species. — What advantage would we have over beasts without language? — Where would our art institutions, schools, and universities be? Through what could the scholars reveal themselves, or even obtain erudition? — I was blind and obdurate, like most who from utter nature and reason are incapable of investigating nature and deny intellectual freedom on a self-made height.

The next day we came together as usual so as to discuss what had been heard and to seek practical evidence where possible. As much as we strove, it just did not work. Grollmann said, "The matter seems to me like a hieroglyph which must be solved first in order to be put into practice." Reineck said, "The matter seems to be to not be impossible, but I believe the solution must come from the practice." I said, "I consider the matter to be neither a puzzle nor a hieroglyph, but new in such a way that we still have trouble believing in it. It was just the same for us with the earlier lessons, they, had we not straightaway found factual evidence, would have remained just as incomprehensible to us. The finer a matter is, the harder it is to analyse; hence I claimed it is our duty to make attempts for as long as until the truth has been put to the test." Everyone gave their agreement and we called upon each other to make attempts, and even if still no results came to light, to think of the old saying: "We will learn through our mistakes."

It is difficult to describe in what a strange situation we found ourselves. Each made an effort to think a word and to give a talk on it, but instead of speaking, we all spontaneously began laughing and could not help ourselves. Grollmann said finally, "Thus it's not working! We must make attempts, otherwise we are like faint-hearted boys who play soldiers and run from one another at the sight of an adult. — I think of the word 'Joseph' and want to seek to talk to it.

Joseph is the name of the foster father of Christ and hence an important word. If we think over the consequences of this fosterage, we are drawn into the origin and the story of the origin of the Christian religion, from which everything arose which it has brought about already on the earth." Here I interrupted him and said, "That leads to nothing. — If the imagined word shall serve as a means of attunement, then we must be able to speak by means of it on anything we like and not only on its historical or assumed meaning." — "That is impossible," Sigmann replied, "in that the imagined word will only ever recall its meaning." I responded, "The instruments by which we attuned ourselves earlier did not prescribe any content. I spoke with the pliers in my hand and did not make the slightest allusion to the instrument." Reineck said, "It is true, the tool for attunement was in none of our attempts the actual content of our talks. — The word which we want to use for our ultimate goal must according to this observation work without meaning, work merely as a power within us, then we can expect results like we had with the former ways of attunement. — But, who can believe in a power of the words without meaning and definition?"

Now we stood again at the old spot. Words without meaning! — Language without sense! — What are they? — Nothing — empty sound! — Thus one said to another; only Bentheim spoke, "Sound is something though and I believe that sound can probably bring forth an effect on our disposition. Music has in itself no meaning, and yet its impact is not to be denied." Sigmann said to this, "Music works as music, as connections of notes which already by themselves have something characteristic, but a mere word without meaning has nothing at all, especially if we do not express it, but merely think it." Bentheim was brought to silence by this rejoinder, for he did not make any further response to it. I seized the initiative and said, "I have no other advice for our embarrassment than to practise thinking words both with and without meaning and, in the case we obtain no success, attuning ourselves through visible tools until we have found a secure basis over the attunement ability through words."

Everybody agreed with this suggestion, and it was decided to make a start straightaway. Grollmann said, "I have in my life often thought about the phrase which you use when you know something which another considers to be a secret, and at the question of where you know it from, answer: my little finger told me. Perhaps this phrase is based on one of the methods in which we have been receiving instruction for a few days; then it would not be grasped out of thin air, but rather contained in nature. I stretch my little finger up in the air and want to have myself attuned for the explanation of the present task.

A word imagined in us should be capable of attuning us to speak about things which we could not even comprehend at all. How is that possible? Does the meaning of the word bring about the attunement, or does the cause lie in a different combination? The word, in the extended sense is language. Should the word of attunement expand our language abilities or give new words? Both cannot be. — Should its meaning lead us to other, perhaps foreign ideas? The association of ideas is a play of the imagination paired with reason. Only such an association is a hidden logical activity which delivers nothing more than an uninterrupted chain of logic which often makes the uneducated as certain as the educated, and it is an innate characteristic of reason. To the extent it would be possible that a word would apart from its meaning have a power or a feature, then an effect could be counted on which would equal that of the visible tools; but the word without meaning dispenses with any feature, hence also any ability to attune." — Here he fell silent for a few moments, but immediately continued again, "I am speaking as well as I can. But whether I am following the mood received through the finger, I do not know, but feel that something more is to be said for which I have no words and no way of expressing."

We all endeavoured to speak, partly with gestures and poses, partly even with tools held in the hand, but every talk failed at the precipice, whether the meaning of the word or the meaningless word was the means of attunement. We lost the hope for the day of obtaining a result, and left it over to the future to gain us information.

***

Seventh Lesson: Necessity of Speaking Freely

In the evening, when we arrived at Mr Rückmann's, we gave him a report of our vain endeavours. He responded, "What you received yesterday is a seed which shall now develop, set root, germinate, and become a fruit bearing plant. Daily practice cannot fail to obtain results even in this area; hence I call upon you to seek steadfastly. Perhaps opportunity will yet be found in the course of our discussions to speak about this topic. Until then I must indicate patience to you. For today I have resolved to talk once more with you about the art of talking freely and to indicate to you on what occasions its use is essential and necessary.

The inducements to speak are indeed not to be counted, nevertheless they are to be grasped under two rubrics. The first sort encloses in itself the common conversation in its unending permutations. The second sort encompasses all the sorts of recitals where you speak about a thing, about important affairs for the education and instruction of others. The first, as insignificant as it may appear, encroaches so much into bourgeois life that it is considered a beneficial bond of the social order. For this reason it is necessary to examine it alone.

The peculiarity of social conversation consists in that it does not concern itself with what you say — rather — how you say it. The matter with which the conversation preoccupies itself is not taken into account at all, to the contrary, it would be the death of open conversation if you wanted to pose a specific task for discussion. Any ever so tiny topic, to the extent it does not lie beyond the bounds of decency, decorum, and morality, can give inducement to speak, the easier and more unforced the language moves, the more it shows of the taste and culture of those speaking. If someone wanted in such company to monopolise the tone for themselves and speak over weighty things, then he would, and even if he were to have said the best things, be considered a man without culture. A similar judgement is offered for those who speak about trivial things with pathos and learned affectation. The spirit of a good conversation, as already stated, does not concern itself with the topic of the conversation, but rather passes with the greatest facility from one to the other, speaks now of a rose, then of an embroidery, there of a painting, here of the song, the next moment over the similarity of a five year old girl to her mother and afterwards of a dress, and all this with a light, fleeting interest where nobody claims to speak or want to speak better than the others, but rather makes their little contribution of their own accord to never let the conversation falter, on the other hand interrupting nobody and not disturbing them in the exercise of their social freedom. Here the moment must attune us and tell us how, what, and for how long we should speak; and if all participants of society move and speak in this spirit, then there is a painting where every figure stands in the proper place, but also none can be taken out without making a gap in the whole. No figure can and may distinguish itself especially, the social activity of all must combine into a single whole where the participants are only members whose main aim it must be to subordinate their independence to the working together of all.

Examples of such a free conversation are encountered frequently in the company of females, who possesses far more courage for abandoning themselves to the natural instinct of language than men. In the higher circles this way of conversing is connected with confident posture and movement, a key trait of good education and upraising. Had a nobleman learnt everything and yet was not in possession of the free language of conversation, he would not be respected by his peers. Here bourgeois society stands far behind the nobility, because there you hear talk of great merit, of learnedness, bourgeois virtues, and classicism, and we are constantly reminded of how insignificant we still are, and how far we still have to equal the posited ideals. Everybody makes themselves important here, everybody wants to stand next to the posited models, even if they are not in a position to pick up a napkin fallen from the table without a racket and great ceremony. The greatest scholar of the bourgeois tone steps into a higher society as though into a strange world whose speech and manners he does not know and cannot imitate, whereas a highly cultured man knows how to find his way in bourgeois society just as easily as in his own. But certainly there is nothing more ridiculous and stiffer than an aped fine tone where you tie freedom up in rules and turn facility into gauche compulsion, where everybody at the table handles the napkins in the same way as the others and leads the knife and fork with the same rhythm and grip to the mouth. Louis XV asked a nobleman, 'Do you hold the fork with your left or right hand when eating meat?' — 'With the right, sir,' the latter answered. — 'Also good,' the king said, 'you are dining today at my table though?' 'I know well,' the nobleman replied, 'that with you, as king of the French and the good tone, it is not about whether you lead the spoon with three or five fingers to your mouth, if you do not just stick it in the sack.' 'Bravo,' the king said, 'you have given my court the most beautiful compliment.'

I have talked about this sort of free speaking at more length than you were perhaps expecting. But the matter obtains an importance in so far as we are required here to value and use language without consideration for the content, but merely as language. Let us leave those great spirits who seek geniality everywhere and also want to shine in social circles with the unseasonable fruits of their understanding; to us it is enough to know that language even without gleaming brilliance, without witty tirades and genial clichés can hold together a society and give the proof that it is capable of binding people without magnificent aura in a social order to each other. To the wise the components of language are those powers wherein he seeks the motions of life; the content of it is to him accidental phenomena which were not unconditionally necessary. Being able to speak, however, is a basic nature of humanity.

To the second type belong such talks that deal with a matter or a generality which you cannot always comprehend without precise discussion. The inducements to them are diverse both in smaller and in larger circles, in churches and schools, at pulpits and altars, in the open field and in closed rooms, where instruction and edification are expected. Here then it is to be investigated with prudence whether we should be attuned by the environment, by visible tools of attunement, by gestures, by imagined objects, or by a word absorbed into us, in order to carry out the intended task. Free speaking is the highest adornment of human nature. When it occupies itself completely with the most sacred interests of humanity, with God, religion, and immortality, then it becomes of a prophetic nature where it penetrates into the secrets of God who, himself word, makes the human through the means of speech into a likeness of himself. Free talk is so essential that you can brazenly claim the Christian church will not entirely secure itself for as long as until the written and previously thought over talks are banished and instead emerge from the mood of the moment. No preacher, to the extent the spirit of Christianity is lived up to, should receive the text for his sermon before he has already entered the pulpit, so that, since preparation and learnedness cannot aid him, he would be forced to seek the mood and, a true champion of God, venture the struggle with all the difficulties of speaking freely. If you, as was already mentioned, believe the first converters of heathens had carried scriptures with them, then you are deceiving yourself — feeling and acknowledging God and his spirit was their only study, and this gave them the power to also unite the most heterogenous beliefs and to obtain them for their doctrine.

Putting this first, we want to look over once more the principles according to which you can learn to feel and acknowledge your life, before we make use of them for Christianity, in order to imprint them more deeply on the memory.

Being able to walk, stand, and speak, these we have declared to be those characteristics of humans which actually make them human and are not to be dispensed with in any position or with any performance. Even such labours as desire a seated position are not excluded here, because even here it is mostly about the deportment of the body and of the limbs. We want to go through these three sorts once more in order, so as to also make clear that which could have escaped us before.

The man shall feel his character and his profession and learn accordingly to walk and stand. With the Greeks, that classic people, the walk was a special trait for the recognition of a man. A man whose gait did not betray a confident rhythm could obtain neither attention nor respect. Some were turned away even before they had stepped up to the rostrum, simply because they approached it with uncertain steps. Those who abased the human form with curvatures and bows were also contemptible to the proud and to despots. Self-importance and pomposity in the gait drew mockery and distrust to it. The human has apart from status, birth, and world circumstances an innate dignity: seek to portray this in your gait, and the path is open to many undertakings.

The art of standing is no less important than that of walking; for it is not only about how, but also about where we stand. If we have to talk with someone, to sort out a matter, then we should not be too distant and not too close. Not too distant in order to not show a lack of courage and trust, not too close so that those with whom we speak still have room to see our figure and posture. The natural distance is the length of a man. The small man may stand somewhat closer than the tall man, but the tall man remains at an appropriate distance in order to not make a mark against his figure and to not embarrass his opposite. The distance increases according to the number of listeners. Feeling will give us here after some practice the certain measure. But once you occupy the place, then claim it without stiffness and arrogance. Gestures of many kinds are not suited for the man of culture, and the orator also abstains from such because they are mostly signs of lack of confidence, of charlatanism, and of the uncertainty of the soul's mood. The gestures should, as we have seen already, attune, but not instruct. Only through practice can the truth of what is said prove its worth, mere pondering will not bring you a step further.

Speaking is the most beautiful, most sublime, but also the most difficult art of human life. It was already said before, however, that under actual speaking is to be understood not monotonous reciting of the usual notices, be it the news of the day or a learned article, but rather the free advancement of our innermost thoughts and feelings. This way of speaking is then a revealing of that state of mind in which the mood has placed us, which takes in everything which sounds around it and develops thoughts and images of which the speaker him-self often had no idea at all previously.

We have discussed five ways of attuning us for the talk and confirmed them by our own evidence:

1) By the impression of the objects and circumstances around us.
2) By the look or touch of any desired tools of attune-ment.
3) By the sleight of our hands and limbs, to the extent they are to be brought into all possible forms, and by the posture and position of the body and the touch of it by fingers and hands.
4) By the idea of such means of attunement by means of our imagination and ability to think.
5) Finally by a word thought within us which awakens and enlivens the speech with elementary power.

The first way of attuning yourself is easy as soon as we pos-sess the power of putting aside previous ideas and sensations and abandoning ourselves to the impressions of the moment.

The second way already offers greater difficulty in that we withdraw from the impressions of the environment and must surrender to the attunement of the chosen tool. The uninhib-itedness is not so easy to claim here in that the objects around us constantly work on our senses and seek to distract us from the tool of attunement. Moreover the content of the talk lies outside the realm of visibility because it contains objects of the imagination and the ability to think, which are very often contrary to our previous views. As soon as we let ourselves be intimidated, the stream of talk is interrupted, our favourite views remain faithful, thus the talk loses its freedom, and we see ourselves easily brought into entangling ourselves in our self-made nooses.

The third class, where we attune ourselves by means of the hands, the fingers, the arms and feet, as well as the posture of the body and the placement of the hands on it, is subject to the same difficulties as the second, only the attention is easily affixed by the activity of your own limbs and the mood and uninhibitedness preserved.

The fourth way of attuning ourselves by imagined tools and gestures is subject to many hindrances because the slightest external phenomenon can distract our attention and destroy our mood. In old stories and images we frequently find this way of attunement, and anyone who is practised in it obtains a mastery over the activity of their imagination which must also be of great advantage in other respects. Anyone who achieves the power of being able to think and imagine what they want will think more thoroughly over any topic and, while others are endeavouring to get a hold of the matter, they will already be at the close of their inquiries.

The fifth way of attuning yourself with words is the keystone of thinking, is the crown of freedom, is the inextinguishable light of the wise, is the so often badly misunderstood philosopher's stone which made fools of so many of the unwise, is the key to the true knowledge of God —

After these recapitulations, I conclude today's lesson and will make the attempt tomorrow to make you aware of the principles of Christianity." — We parted, without assembling the next morning on the deck, in that each sought to affix in their memory for themselves alone what had been heard up until then.

***

Eighth Lesson: Beginning of Creation

In the evening we met punctually at Mr Rückmann's. We were full of expectation of seeing Christianity illuminated philosophically in his way, and asked him, when we had barely finished eating, to give us his lecture over the most important point of our existence.

He began immediately and said, "In order to learn to appreciate a matter appropriately, it is above all necessary to distinguish the essential from the accidental and the unchangeable from the changeable. Hence the question arises: is the Christian religion a product of time, or does it have its roots in eternity? — In the first case history must give us information; in the second only the knowledge of God, who alone is eternal, can provide us with instruction. But where do we find the root which clings to eternity? — On which path is it to be sought, and by which features to be recognised? — The Bible, that canonical book, shows us, in that it leads us to Paradise, a primitive condition, a first man, and instructs us to thus fathom the need of humanity.

You will instinctively ask here how such an investigation is possible, since in this respect the historical evidence does not suffice. Here it must be said: what history is not capable of, reason, in a word philosophy, must do. The true philosophy needs no history in that none is based so certainly as to be able to build unconditionally on it. It is accordingly a perverse procedure to want to establish through history philosophical truths, since the latter must be indubitably true, but the former is never raised beyond any doubt. History can be reinforced by philosophy, but philosophy never by history.

I know well that such a procedure is not easy, and most prefer to subordinate themselves to historical authorities in order, supported on these, to reach their goal with comfortable steps. — But it is not made so comfortable for the human. — The creator no more gave him reason for nothing than he gave him seeing, hearing, feeling, and tasting. We must think, penetrate through our reason to the origin, then we raise ourselves to where we see God and nature in us as if in a mirror and are no longer required to satisfy ourselves with theses and hypotheses.

In order to come in this way to a goal, it is necessary to hold ourselves to what we see, feel, and hear, what is infallible and unchallenged and what remains. But what is that? It seems an almost superfluous question, because each person sees creation and the countless creations around themselves. Surely in this way we have a certainty, an indissoluble thing which, if we understand how to build on it, rests on a foundation which does not sway and does not yield, and even if a thousand storms threaten to destroy it.

Creation exists. — How did it become? This is now the second question which forces or has already forced itself on everyone. If this question is so rarely answered completely, the blames lies not in the matter at hand, but rather on our inertia and changeability which hinders us in thinking about it, also on the faint-heartedness to find something where others, just as sluggish and faint-hearted as us, sought in vain. The ability to think, to consider, and to make judgements raises the human to *a proper* species and puts him in a position to think about his origin and the aim of his existence. — This capability raises him above the beasts, who indeed often develop a cleverness and skilfulness which puts the human to shame, on the other hand showing no traces of the presence of a free will. And yet the human belongs to the class of the becoming, like everything which we see around us as vegetation and life. 'How did that happen?', the human asks, 'and in what hierarchy does it all relate together?'

When we consider the reason for the creation of earthly creatures, we must at first investigate whether the earth has existed for eternity, or has arisen in time. The earth is a composed object, something brought into a specific form. The composed object can disintegrate, and the form change, accordingly the eternal existence of the earth is already doubtful. If the earth cannot remain in existence for eternity, then it is also not of eternity, thus it belongs in the class of the becoming like every other thing which we see on it.

74

The earth is materially eternal, the form subject to transience. If this is so, then the sun, moon, and stars must likewise be shapes of time and have a reason for creation. But what is eternal, if the earth, sun, moon, and stars are not? — Nothing is undeniably eternal but space, which was never begun, is never-ending, and by its expansion likewise contains the concept 'eternity' within itself. In this we must, as soon as we want to get to work rationally and philosophically, seek the origin of all worlds, all powers and capabilities.

Will space, before there were the sun and stars, have surely been empty? That is unthinkable, otherwise no celestial bodies could have arisen in it. But what power built the celestial bodies, gave them form and the paths in which they find themselves? — Such power can have been nothing else but a mobile-living spirit which fermenting and working from eternity pushes the raw matter from itself like the wine from the yeast. This spirit is therefore the original divine spirit, is the paternal power from which everything arises and by which everything which is there has become. But in what way, or with what means does this spirit work? That is now the question.

Apollo's system of tones reigns in the air, in the ether, and in all bodies, hard or soft, large or small. This system of tones must therefore also have been contained in space from eternity fermenting as a spiritual power of action. If we consider here the investigations of thoughtful music teachers, it is found that the vibrations of the tones rest on specific motions and even on specific forms which are depicted as precisely as when the draughtsman brings lines and angles onto paper. Now it is to be asked: is the system of tones the highest thing we know in creation, or is there yet a purer power, a more distinguished vibration from which the wondrous phenomena of creation could arise? As wonderful as it is to know the visible creation, all its parts and even the space in which it all moves is purely and systematically tuned, nobody will deny though that thought, free will, that is, language or the word from which thought and free will come, must stand not much higher than the tones and harmonies of Apollo. The *word* or *language* is the highest which the human recognises in creation, and hence he must seek in language everything which

God brings forth, if he wants to proceed logically and according to his reason.

The highest characteristic of the human, which we must consider to be the source of all his splendid gifts of understanding, reason, regulated feelings, and the independence of his nature, is according to all which we have said and heard contained in language. The realm of Apollo has shown itself in space, in the ether, in the air, in nature, and in all parts of creation. — To the extent we are now in a position to recognise language in the same way and to just such an extent, we have the basic cause of human knowing, wanting, and feeling not only in us, but in known creation as the word and, since then the word is God, God in the word. — In this eternal confession of faith, in this basic concept of all knowing, in this eternally living philosophy which is at the same time the original principle of all religions, the original religion itself, we have for our investigations found a positive goal whose sight preserves us from every confusion and every deception.

In order to get to know the being of language or the word in nature, we must first know that every individual letter, that is every sound, has its characteristic primitive form belonging only to it. — This primitive form is not fixed to any distance or any extent; it pours from star to star, from cloud to cloud, from mountain to mountain, from tree to tree, from stone to stone, from creature to creature, from limb to limb until in the innermost folds of the heart and all the internal and external organs of the body. If we learn to feel this vocalisation in ourselves, then the spirit of God is given to us, and we connect ourselves to the eternal power of creation which, like us, can think everything, want everything, and, to the extent it is without limits, can accomplish everything."

Here Mr Rückmann made a pause. Since none of us made as if to say something, he continued, "I have led you to the beginning of creation, have plunged you into the chaos which was preceding the creation, but which was pregnant with all the creatures and parts of creation. Seek to collect yourself in it, to seek and to find your own self through the indicated means, only then will you be in a position to get to know the determinations of life in general and the duties of your self-chosen profession."

This lecture had made such an impression on us that we really did find ourselves in a chaos and also saw no hope yet of freeing ourselves from it. We finally obtained the composure to express ourselves over what we had heard and to have ourselves corrected on a few points. When the hour of departure came, we went off quietly to our rest in order to let the received ideas, like the first spirit of creation in the chaos, ferment within us.

***

The Students in Chaos

When we had assembled on the deck the next morning, the same darkness as the day before seemed to still lie over us; for nobody had the courage or the uninhibitedness to touch the previous day's topic. I was finally ashamed of this mood and said, "My friends! What we heard yesterday is so strange to us that we are as if looking into a different world. I ask, if we found ourselves at once transported from this ship to an unfamiliar region, would it surely be expedient not to discuss our state and at the same time to investigate the area? We are in a new state, are in a chaos from which we must free ourselves. Our teacher has put in our hands various means for free inquiry, so that it would be childish not to use them and instruct ourselves over the essentials of his lecture yesterday. We are in the dark, in an unreflective chaos. I ask you to let yourselves be attuned by this idea and seek a light by reciprocal talks which will show us the exit from this seemingly impenetrable labyrinth."

Everybody approved this suggestion of being attuned by the said idea, and Sigmann, after he had composed himself for about a minute, began.

"I am in chaos. All around me there is nothing but dark mist. No detail, no spark of light shimmers for me; but I feel myself in this enormous emptiness. To where can I get, where will I seek an exit? It is to me as if my entire being wanted to disintegrate and melt away in the mist. That is the terrible warning which I draw from the chaos, to indeed not let myself disintegrate. The world is also a chaos, still more terrible than that state preceding the creation because here deceptive lights shimmer which beguile the senses, heart, and mind and lead us onto paths which, instead of to life, lead into an abyss where we are lost forever. Hence I say, God took it on himself to draw us from the first chaos; it is our duty to free ourselves from the chaos of the world and to win back the pure human nature."

We accorded our friend the most sincere thanks indeed for his talk, although we easily saw that he had distanced himself from the goal instead of getting nearer to it. Mr Rückmann spoke expressly about the first chaos in which we should have composed ourselves and gone forth from. Sigmann, however, used this idea as an image in order to make pure, moral reflections, and had led us, instead of out of, into a doubled chaos. — We asked amongst each other for a new attempt, but nobody could manage it. A few stood up, applied various means of attunement, but even if a free thought wanted to appear, it seemed to be shooed away again by the self-consciousness of our views, or by prejudices which we had assumed from incomplete explanations of the creation story as it is portrayed in Genesis. We absolutely could not arrive at any result and decided to confess our inability to Mr Rückmann and ask him for further explanations. We parted with the mutual assurance of not letting the matter rest, but applying all to shedding light on the chaos.

***

Ninth Lesson: In the Chaos there is Light

Evening arrived. We arrived punctually, and when we had finished eating, we revealed to Mr Rückmann our situation. He was not astonished, by contrast he said it would have surprised him to see us any differently than we were. "I will attempt," he continued, "to explain to you my views, which are supported by the evidence of the ancient wise men and by nature, as clearly as possible. Only I must ask for your patience with my project, for rescuing from the night or from the maelstrom of the sea is harder than leaping in. So listen!

We think back to the eternal chaos where everything lies still mixed up together, where no detail, no being, no special power has separated from the whole. All is just one, like milk where neither cream, butter, whey, nor water have separated from one another. Thus lies the chaos, the infinite space filled with the material of future worlds and creatures, there in inexorable fermentation and showing yet no light and no form. Now the coarser parts separate from the finer, draw together, and celestial bodies arise, draw everything of the same kind to themselves and give the fermentation a specific direction. But at this the fleeting, the purer and living being in space has become still more fleeting and spiritual, it stirs, labours, works and creates, also pushes that which is too full of light and fire from itself, drives it to the fortress of heaven where, driven by the rotation of the eternal word, it places itself as a luminous sphere in space and prepares day and night and the seasons. In this way two worlds have formed, the world of coarse matter and that of fiery light. The being in space has through this magnificent precipitation maintained its temperature and now ferments much more calmly and judiciously according to the plan of the word speaking in it and forms on the coarser substratum plants, animals, and humans. — Suns and earths stand in their special places, but act through space on one another and produce and give birth in this way uninterruptedly to new creatures. Earth, water, air, and fire have separated so that each comprises a realm described by a definite border or stronghold, but unite incessantly and deliver material for new creations. Everything is active, everything in creation seems to have found the life course of its destiny, and the lively fleeting spirit of space flies commandingly from world system to world system and breathes breath into its chosen races, on earth humanity, so that the created serves the spirit of creation as it were as a channel in order to penetrate through all parts of creation and return again in humanity to itself.

Only, on what paths does this spirit come, and on which does it return? Which is the first and which is the last step of this wondrous course? The plant kingdom precedes the animal kingdom, and the animal kingdom precedes humanity; indeed, from the plant kingdom actually everything emerges which we see on earth in the realm of the living.

Plants are not created, but rather reproduced through the influence of light which, combined with air and water, sinks down to the earth. The seed for all plants is contained so infallibly in nature that here already the most unambiguous tests have long since been made and can be made at any time. — Nature sprouts grass and herbs, trees and shrubs without any assistance. Indeed, you might claim their origin is not actually an act of creation, but rather an entirely natural transformation of the coarse into finer things, and then a stepping back to the primal matter. — Nature is, and hence everything must be, as it is because it turns about itself constantly in its transformations. Since this, according to all experiences which we are capable of making, cannot be denied, creation stands thus finished before us and we have merely to investigate in which way animals and humans could arise.

Grass, herbs, shrubs and trees are present as components of nature. We see the first phenomena of life in slimy water and fermenting, damp matter; only we do not yet recognise any rule by which living beings develop here. We make the first and safest experiences over this in meadows which are covered in foliage or other things, often teeming with insects. Each of these animals is a stalk of grass come to life which, hindered in its development, became an animal. The way this happened is explained in the following manner.

We make the observation of trees that their growth always arises from nodes which at autumn, or by the interruption of growth, form by means of other hindrances. As soon as the sap surges in spring from the roots into the young sapling, the nodes open, and a new shoot puts forth and continues to grow until autumn arrives again or the appearance of a new hindrance. In a similar way the branches also arise and likewise grow. Now as soon as the node on the young branch, or even sometimes already on the first trunk become too fixed and strong, then instead of a new shoot, a fruit develops. This is accordingly the consequence of an apparent irregularity in that the main direction of the tree seems to aim at a constant growth. Only nature performs both by itself in that it sprouts there a branch and here a fruit. As the new shoots of a young sapling and the branches of a grown tree arise from nodes, so does it come about with the first germination and branches of each plant which develops either to a new stalk or branch, or to a fruit or flower containing seeds. — Germinating, growing, forming a node, and resting in order to grow anew or put forth fruit is the business of every plant. If now in the last case the stalk of grass is hindered in its growth by a light cover that does not avert dampness and warmth, the roots force despite this the collected nourishment into the covered and oppressed stalk, increase the fermentation in the already present nodes, become purer and purer, open new channels, separate and purify the nodes for as long as until an animal-like organisation is formed, frees itself from the pressure which burdens it, and hops as an insect, as a grass come to life into the light of day. The origin of the maggot and caterpillars by an obstructed development of the blossom into fruit is a truth confirmed from experience by every countryman over a long time already. According to this analysis it would not be difficult for me to explain to you the type of origin of most animals. But I will satisfy myself with having made you aware of the origin of the lower types of animal, and just add that the variety of climates is also the cause of the variety of animal species. If we to this end consider yet the natural change of locality, for example, mountain and valley, forests and meadows, rivers and lakes, then the number of animal species cannot surprise us anymore, but the thought of the simplicity of this activity of creation drives us to admiration and worship.

After all this, it is to be asked by which hindrances and developments did humanity surely arise? No mortal seems to have ever seen this, notwithstanding that all mythologies aim at such a manner of arising. The Brahmans consider the lotus to be the channel for the arising of humanity — the Germans the oak. A large party of the educated accept the acacia. Be it as one wishes, it is beyond doubt that here a two-fold, perhaps three, four, or five-fold hindrance must have been in the way in order to bring forth the perfections which we see in humanity. — We have seen by what gradation the plants bring to light results through visible hindrances — the first gradation is new growth through forming a node. — The second consists of the development of nodes to a fruit. With the third gradation the fruit is hindered in its development and develops into a living animal. — The fourth and last gradation finally arises from a hindrance which burdens the developing animal which, purified by the purest process of fermentation, grasps with the hands about itself and appears in an erect posture. —

Creation with all its parts and creatures now lies before us. — Be the plan which I have drawn up also still so small, it can though give us an idea of the beginning of all things and their intertwining effects. It remains for us after this only to investigate with what means everything which we have examined has brought that forth in order to then go over to our main task, the discussion of the Christian religion and its basic principles. Since the time does not allow us anymore to start on a new topic, we will conclude the evening with what has just been said."

We left, each occupied with his thoughts about the content of the day's lecture according to his individual views, and went to bed, without allowing ourselves any judgement, so as to be able to give a hearing to our thoughts undisturbed.

***

The First Light in the Darkness

When we had assembled the next morning, everybody sought to express their astonishment over what had been heard the day before. Grollmann finally got a word in and said, "What we heard yesterday is new in such a way that I would have considered anyone who had said to me a few days ago that I would hear such an explanation over the story of creation to be a dreamer. Mr Rückmann has presented to us the entire act of creation as if he had been present himself at the beginning. He, this wise man, this philosopher, analyses the efficacy of the creator with such confidence as one has with the needs of day-to-day company. Everything is clear in his view, he is master of everything and makes his syllogisms not merely with common antecedent and posterior clauses, which are mostly still very obscure, but rather with irrevocable natural powers whose results stand factually before our eyes." Bentheim asked after this for permission to speak and continued in the following way.

"Without getting too close to Mr Rückmann, our magnificent teacher, I must confess that I am still very much in doubt about his manner of origin for humanity. — You all know my unconditional belief in the canonical truths of the Bible. Now I must say that his views deviate much too much from the creation of the first Biblical humans to be able to agree with them. There it states: And the Lord God formed man of the dust of the ground[*]. According to Rückmann he arose from a tree. Since these two views never unite, I must confess with regret that I will preserve my own belief here against that of our teacher." — Sigmann interrupted him and said, "I have often thought about the creation of humans according to the literal sense of the Bible, and never found a certain conclusion. Dust of the ground[†], I said to myself, is something gathered artificially with visible hands and tools. But since it is not to be thought that God to this end transformed himself into the form of a common labourer, the matter always re-

---

[*]   [Tr.: Genesis 2:7.]
[†]   [Tr.: note that Luther's German translation of the Bible refers to a clod of earth rather than dust of the ground.]

mained a puzzle to me. According to Rückmann's explanation every uncertainty is put aside. — God creates, that is, he lets become and grow. The tree is something sprouting from the earth, thus nothing more than the dust of the ground. From such, from dust of the ground becoming a tree, God created according to eternal laws of vegetation the human, and breathed into his nostrils the breath of life*. Truly, if Mr Rückmann had not expressed any truth but this, we would have to give thanks and admiration to him as a rare man gifted with the highest knowledge of nature." —

When a small pause occurred here, Reineck continued, "Our friend Sigmann has spoken so much from my own heart that I feel urged to express my warmest thanks to him. — God lets become. — God lets grow. With these two phrases his entire efficacy is expressed. He does not compose, model, and hammer, and yet everything is in the greatest perfection. According to simple, divine basic laws he produces everything and lets the human grow according to his eternal plan. The tick among the grass, the caterpillar on the tree, they all have the organs of the human; why should what happens so frequently in miniature and before our eyes not also be able to take place in the large? The human was grown, with this conviction too, the history of the world becomes clear to me in that I can imagine in this way in every heavenly sphere, in every climate a first man."

In this sense we spoke for a long time and discussed the matter so thoroughly that finally Bentheim declared himself in agreement with us, and we looked forward in advance to the present evening more than ever before.

***

---

*   [Tr.: cf. Genesis 2:7.]

Tenth Lesson: Sound and Word

Hardly had we assembled in the evening with Mr Rückmann and enjoyed some food, than he continued in his instruction.

"After we have seen everything become, we want to also investigate by what powers it was brought forth. — We had to start with nothing but chaos, that is, an eternal, infinite space in which everything that now is still rested unformed. Space is still, even if filled with celestial bodies, infinite as always. In space two powers showed themselves which could not be created because they exist independently of time, place, and matter in themselves, these are: the harmony of the sounds and the relationships of the word. — The harmony of the sounds rests on the attunement of the ether, on the elastic fleeting being which flows in space. The truth that every sound forms on glass plates, strings, and other instruments by means of its vibrations an innate, unalterable form before the eyes has been demonstrated by Professor Chladni[*] before the eyes of all Germany irrefutably. On this is founded the following conclusion:

> If every sound has its specific form for the eye, then every form has its peculiar sound, but which cannot be heard, but rather only felt.

This basic principle is of the highest importance. It is not enough that thereby the three main components of life — seeing, hearing, and feeling — must be thought to be in complete interaction and agreement, the doctrine of the old Rabbis, that God himself had Adam written, obtains an entirely natural interpretation; for if every sound is form, and every form is a felt sound, then the actual system of notes lies in nature, and we have God himself as the teacher to watch writing the

---

[*] [Tr.: Ernst Chladni (1756–1827), German physicist and musician who did pioneering work on acoustics and on the origin of meteorites.]

notes. As soon as these sentences can be comprehended and not refuted, we are on the trail of the power which made everything which is made.

In the word are contained not only all the forms of the sounds, but they increase themselves by the different sound of the vowels, by the most diverse interruptions by means of the consonants, and finally by the artful fusing of letters into syllables and words. — In the word are found all the forms of geometry. — Every vowel has in addition to its tone form a peculiar sound form by means of which the vowels form their scale not only in height and depth of the harmonic relationships, but according to their original sounds. In this way we have a wealth which is immeasurable; and since the sound form is expressed far more definitely and distinctly than the tone form, it must act still much more powerfully on our feelings and enliven them for free speaking.

In order to make the matter clear, you may consider just the sounds of the five basic vowels differentiated with the greatest clarity — i, e, o, u, a — against the imperfect sounds of musical instruments which are always heard in the imperfect sounds ue, oe, and ao (as long o). You have to give every praise to the musicians who despite the imperfection of the elements produced the system of tones in full and exhaustively; by contrast you must be highly astonished that the scholars, the so-called philosophers, lost the system of a sound scale completely and in their blindness even denied the traces by which they could have again arrived at some certainty. — In the word is the creative power. The word is the highest thing in creation. — Be the gleam of the red sunrise yet so glorious, be the evening sky yet so beautiful, higher than everything in creation stands the power which names the glories of nature and is able thereby to make them our possession. God is the eternal word, and therefore creation is its realm. God is the creative word, and therefore the plan of creation lies already in advance in the word, and God is therefore will and power and wisdom at the same time.

In the word all forms are contained. — Every vowel has its original form befitting only it and which appears through composition in infinite modifications. If this is the case, then every form must also be a word which expresses itself

86

through vibrations in our feelings. — The chaos was in the state of fermentation. Fermentation is a dissociation of the coarser from the purer and spiritual, as we distinctly see with wine. The spiritual spreads in the state of fermentation into crooked and straight lines, into angles and arcs through the infinite receptacle, space, obtains dominance and stirs, formed by relationships of form into the word, into innate, free activity of life. — In this way the highest trait of the universe, the word, continues to act and weave in its eternal lines, forms, and vibrations, and since the coarser parts, even if driven by its power, remain surrounded and penetrated by it, they retain in the formation the character of the word, roll themselves into the innate point, place themselves into specific lines and angles to other points and draw in these relationships the letters of the creative word of God into nature and its creatures.

After what has been said, it behooves us principally to hear the word not only as sound, but to learn to see and feel it as form. The primal forms of the letters have been lost in common life in such a way that you consider the entire matter to be a phantasm of deceived dreamers or frauds. Notwithstanding this, such primal forms are present in nature, and anyone can, if he does not eschew the time and effort, put it to the test. It only remains to be asked accordingly, in what way is it possible to recognise such primal forms again?

The mechanic, when he gets a look at a previously unseen mechanism, investigates its purpose, and its individual parts, and assesses thereby the instruments and means with which those can be made, and puts himself in this way into the position to build a similar mechanism. Thus and in no other way must we also proceed. — The work stands before our eyes, and no envious creator hinders us from looking at it on all sides. Only the mere gazing in wonder is of no use here; we must strive to recognise the means with which the whole could be built thus and in no other way. — We see lines, arcs, points, and angles, see the change of the days and years and the infinite space of the heavens sown with countless worlds. But this immeasurability rests on lines, arcs, and angles, its efficacy on the vibrations of forms as word and in the gradations of light. — Lines, arcs, and angles are therefore our elements in which we have to seek, and should the circumstances of nature be too great for us to investigate, then nobody hinders us from proceeding like the astronomers and bringing the objects of our investigation in a diminished measure as close to us as possible. — The astronomer draws the immeasurable heavens on a piece of paper, and calculates the course of the sun and stars to the second. Thus the researcher, when he is serious about finding the truth, lets the lines, arcs, and angles vibrate in his inner-being, and measures, like the astronomer does the heavens, the bounds between time and eternity.

Over the possibility of seeing sound and word with the eye and feeling them in the disposition, much has already been spoken; the stubborn doubter is, however, not to be helped, to the uninhibited the following serves for their satisfaction. — A musician takes a piece of music in the hand, goes through it with his eyes, without making a sound by himself, or moving his mouth, and specifies the content and the worth of such a thing in the most definite way. Another learns entire folios, absorbs into himself the entire history of the world and a part of its scientific systems, without uttering a word or opening his mouth to speak. Are these not factual proofs that the eye is capable of seeing the word and transferring it into our disposition and ability to think? After such discussions nobody will find it too daring to see such sentences put up as basic results.

Form is word, and light is word.

Every fermentation is a liberation of light from darkness, or a separation of coarser matter from the finer and spiritual.

Every activity of light happens through radiation, consequently through the formation of lines, arcs, and angles.

The entire universe is a great ring, an immeasurable sphere, and thereby a form, a word element.

The word is living, forever active, and creates without rest and standing still.

Lines, arcs, and angles are the roots of the word and sprout the branches of life and of motion through worlds and life systems.

The word steps out in the coarser matter and becomes sound and meaning for the visible sense.

God speaks and the human speaks.

God has himself given himself to the human, and through that the human can rise to the word of feeling where he feels the primal types and hears the language of God.

In this way the human stands at the peak of the glory of God and is capable of documenting with sensory tools the nature of God and thereby obtaining spiritual freedom and immortality.

To the thinking human it is not enough to just surmise a thing, he strives for certainty. Now he asks himself, in what way is an eternal life to be obtained?

We have found the elements of the word in eternal space, and since this has neither in respect of time nor locality any limit, in eternity. When we strive to feel these elements in their form and efficacy, we bear the unmistakeable seal of eternity in ourselves and are in reduced measure what the primal word is in the infinite whole.

You learn music usually on an instrument, but as soon as you have once learnt it thoroughly the instrument is no longer essential, then you carry the music within yourself. For a few indeed the throat and mouth serves as an instrument, only these are likewise seen as external tools because the entire effect emanates externally. But let a complete musician loses hearing and speech, the music will continue to live in his feelings, and none of its countless turning will be lost to him. Thus the word! — Throat, tongue, teeth, and lips are the tool to make use of it externally, but as soon as the elements and the turnings of language once stir in our inner-being and are revealed, then may the external speech organs fall mute, the hearing be lost, in the inner-being the living language remains and will not die anymore, even if the body dissolves into atoms.

But how is the word to be recognised in its primal forms? And through what do we receive the conviction that we have it not only in the mouth, in the instrument directed outwardly, but in our inner-being? — The mouth is the tool for the external world, but it is also the organ of procreation for the inner life. — The human is accustomed as he speaks outwardly to speaking inwardly, and he will soon feel unquestionable results. — God blows the living breath into the nose of the human, says the story of creation*. If you attempt, instead of unseasoned air, to breathe vowels, then words, and finally entire sentences and have the entire body penetrated by them, then you will soon experience what it means to surrender yourself to chance, or nourish yourself with the air of life. If you have come in this way to feeling your inner life distinctly, then you may breathe in questions, and in breathing out expect the answer.

What has just been said should be a book for clarity; to the most earnest will, few words are enough. — We have above already spoken about the word as a means of attunement. — Here it is not only means, but rather power, and therefore those who are attuned by it have not only a guide and helper, no, they draw with their own hands from the primal stream and appropriate the created at will."

Here Mr Rückmann fell silent. — Since none of us made as if to say anything, he drank a gulp of wine and continued.

"I have spoken a lot. Too much, to the extent that you see what has been said merely as shimmering ideas and allow yourselves to play with them. Adequate, as soon as you have the courage to open your soul to eternity, for taking into yourself the idea of infinite space and the universe and seeing yourself as a citizen of this immeasurability. Anyone who starts up their inquiries in the eternity and penetrates outwardly through all the intervals to themselves, they will also find the way back again. — Self-knowledge leads to truth; self-knowledge, however, is not to be obtained to the extent we do not know our origin. Through self-knowledge we learn God and through knowledge of God we recognise ourselves because the human bears the word of God just as infallibly in himself as God himself." —

After this lecture, I took up the conversation, and said, "We thank you, our paternal teacher, for the sharing of these sublime views. If you see us in astonishment, then it is not only the matter, but also your courage in expressing it which is to blame. Why do they not give everybody whose profession it is to spend time on the sciences such an outline? Why do they let them chew for years on proffered, often falsely inter-

---

*   [Tr.: cf. Genesis 2:7.]

preted things without showing them the source from which everything is drawn, and to which everything must return again? — How many doubts and labours would one be relieved of if one knew the foundation on which everything rests and must rest, if one does not want to only build houses of cards? We thank you with honest hearts and promise to never make ourselves unworthy of your teaching."

He offered me his hand, and replied, "I thank you for your undertaking and am assured that your friends will reaffirm it, and plead to this eternal word power which is in us, around us, and everywhere, which wants only to be sought in order to be found, may it illuminate and protect you on the fateful path of your life."

Only a little more was said; for the time when we usually tended to leave was already past, hence we left our teacher with the most unmistakeable expressions of our reverence.

We spoke only a little more amongst one another. But Grollmann said, "If I succeed in ordering in my head what we heard today and planting it in my feelings, then I will think myself wiser than a king to whom the whole world belonged."

***

Recapitulation

When we had assembled on the deck the next day, our closest attention went to repeating what had been heard the day before and imprinting it as much as possible on our memory. — As easily comprehensible to us as the matter had seemed during the lecture, it was difficult for us the next day to find our way into it again. After I, Grollmann, and Reineck had endeavoured in vain to find the connection again through a few baselines, Sigmann spoke.

"In order to make it possible for me to think about what was heard yesterday, I noted down the following points especially:

1) Every tone has its specific form, can therefore also be seen and felt.
2) The tone of the word is sharper than that of music in that it is attuned precisely and distinguished as sound. — The form of the sound expresses itself considerably,

and on this basis the word can likewise be seen and felt like the tone.

3) God is the word, therefore the word is also God. If this is so, then the plan of creation lay already from the beginning in the word, because in it all forms are contained.

4) The mechanic thinks at the sight of an artificial mechanism at first over its aim, and then over the means which which it is produced.

5) The work of creation lies before us. What is its aim? And with what means is it produced?

6) The word has created creation and its parts just as they are.

7) The knowledge of the word is necessary.

8) On the instrument you learn music. By means of the mouth we learn to speak.

9) If music has gone into our inner-being, may the instrument also break, we remain nonetheless musicians. — If the language has come alive in our inner-being, may the mouth also disappear, the spirit will continue to speak, and we remain in it what we were.

I drew up these principles, and will digest them in my head and disposition for as long as until they have become my property, and I can speak and think within myself without the external tool of the mouth."

We expressed our honest joy over the statement of the described points, and each asked him to be permitted to copy them down. He promised it to me with the greatest readiness and confessed that he had not only written down the lectures of Mr Rückmann, but also those talks of ours, as well as his memory had allowed. He continued, "I am not of such lively spirit as you, my friends, and must therefore make use of pen and pencil, diligence and persistence in order to keep up with you." — This unfeigned utterance of modesty impelled us to assure him of our most honest recognition and friendship. Indeed, I made the confession to him that I myself had seen it necessary to keep a diary over the lessons received and their results, and that it would be for us extremely profitable to compare and contrast our labours at a more convenient time. Everybody rejoiced over this and hoped to get the greatest advantage from the recapitulation of them. Still more was spoken over it until each commenced his special business.

***

Eleventh Lesson:
Transition to the Doctrine
of Christianity

In the evening we arrived in a cheerful mood at Mr Rück-mann's. When we had enjoyed some food, he got ready to continue the lessons and said, "We have previously spoken about the vibration of the tone. Since the sound of the word is still far more discriminating than the common tone of music, its vibration must also express still greater effectiveness. — The force of vibration of the tone, since you can daily gather experience over it, is to be spoken of with confidence. Thus I once entered a concert hall whose floor and walls trembled and windows rattled when you played the D string on the double bass just somewhat strongly. I asked the musician about the cause of this conspicuous effect, and he gave as an answer: the hall is tuned to the key of D. I expressed my doubt about this, but he stuck to his claim and played other notes with still greater power than before, and nothing stirred, but barely had he sounded the D than again the entire hall shook. I thought about the phenomenon without getting any more astute than the musician made me. I asked a natur-alist. He seemed to be short of an answer, but suggested the effect arose from the vibration of the air. I sought out my mu-sician again, had the D played for me in the same hall re-peatedly, but did not find the slightest movement in the air. Another time I made the same observation in a church whose walls, windows, and altar trembled when a certain note was struck. It is not the air, I now thought with confidence, which brings forth such effects, in that these walls also did not shake with the most violent storms. I asked the choirmaster about the cause of this phenomenon. He said it is the church tone which makes the entire church tremble. — By means of the air, I asked? No, he replied, by the vibration of the note agree-ing with the building, which is like a spirit in the air, or rather in the ether. — I thanked him for this instruction, and truly, it gave me enough to think about.

When we transfer these observations to the effects of the word, which is subject yet deeper, hidden even more spiritually in the raw elements, to a still far more effective vibration, we have at once a divine power which shook the chaos, built worlds, drew stars into their paths, and can complete everything which we see complete around us. — If we now consider that the word acts the same as sound and form, and we are required to derive the phenomena of attraction from these forms, then the doctrine is established, and we may from the sentences spoken above — if the word is form, then the form is also word — draw the further conclusion that if a tone is in a position to shake walls, the sound of the word must be capable of moving mountains.

Tone and sound strengthen their efficacy in inverse relationship so that with the tone the vibration has a stronger effect from the tone, but with the sound it has a stronger effect from the form.

This is the actual riddle of the Sphinx, the simple, but deeply hidden secret of God and nature. Cleverness cannot solve it, but to the simple disposition it was always unlocked. You hear a tone, and the vibration is stronger as though you were thinking according to the form. Think, however, of the form of a Latin A or O, and the vibration acts stronger, as if you were saying it. — The word acts as deeply hidden as the sanctum of God; the tone is indeed also a component of the word, but, in love with the sense, it flutters about it with lovely melodies. Anyone who can grasp it, grasps it. There is coming perhaps a time when you will be capable of expressing it more clearly; until then each must seek it in themselves and treat it as a self-obtained possession.

We have in this way elaborated the word as power and not as description of a concept, and therefore I believe I can now pass over to and show the principles of Christian religion, in what agreement they stand with what has been said, and to what extent their basic principles are to be derived from those original determinations.

The basic concept of the Christian religion is the trinity of God under the designations of father, son, and spirit.

The father is the eternal primal power already contained in chaos and creating and governing as word form.

The son is the revealing of this power by means of creation and the creatures contained it it, especially humanity.

The spirit is the primal word flowing through creation, collecting in humans, and recognised by them, and emanating from them.

These three potencies are one, as much as worldly cleverness bristles against it and seeks to separate them. The father, as eternal power, must communicate himself to humanity, and this is only possible through his word which he placed in the son whose spirit collects this word and binds it with his power. And consequently the father is perfectly contained in the being of the son and of the spirit.

The pillars of the Christian church are faith, hope, and love. — Believing in the eternal power of the father, in his revelation through the word, and finally believing in the revitalisation of humanity through awakening of the spirit by means of the word which emanates from the father and son.

The *faith* fills us with *hope* for eternal life and awakens in us the *love* for the father, for the word, and for the spirit.

The three main virtues of the Christian are: praying — fasting — giving alms. — The true Christian must pray frequently without though making many words*. His prayer must unite itself with the inner-being so that the sounds of the primal word awaken in order to come by that to true knowledge. — He should fast, that means *live in moderation*, so that the powers of the spirit are not suppressed by delights of the flesh. Giving alms is that activity by means of which he opens the disposition and keeps it receptive for all purely human virtues.

These basic concepts, pillars, and virtues make up the Christian because they express themselves only in his doctrine with such confidence and purity.

‘I baptise you in the name of the father and of the son and of the holy spirit’ is the formula of the priest with which he takes the person to be baptised into the community of the Christian church; and truly, anyone who learns to compre-

---

*   [Tr.: cf. Matthew 6:7.]

hend in these three designations the eternal plan of creation has a signpost which will lead him safely through the storms of the night and the valley of death.

A key distinction of the Christian religion is its foundation which was already laid according to the historical doctrinal concept in eternity, in God. — The cornerstone of the foundation lies in Paradise, with the origin of the first human, where the prophetic word made itself known and augured a messiah. — The promise came down through Israelite history ever more clearly and urgently, until finally the time appeared when the prophecies were fulfilled. — From these few things we see that the Old and New Testaments of the Bible form only one edifice, only one system which is connected in the past with the primal beginning, illuminates the present through its light, and opens from its prophetic power the doors of the future.

It is certainly difficult to connect the threads of the Christian religion to the first created Adam in Paradise; this is the point which has already brought forth much disputation and confusion amongst those of a Christian confession, because the story does not want to agree in considering Adam to be the first of all humans. It is certainly true; to the extent the story of Adam should be accepted as unalterable cornerstone of the Christian religion, admittedly numerous doubts remain. Only if we have in mind the story of the Jews and at the same time consider that they are the only ones who begin with a first human and continue his family tree, then it is not to be wondered that they are seen to be placed as the only connecting thread for spiritual researches. Had we several such stories, the foundation would certainly be more secure; but since this is not the case, we must hold ourselves to what is present and conclude from this the generality and reliability of a primal law. — Adam was a first human, that means sprouted directly from the earth by the seed of God. May other nations have then had their first human, their Adam, whenever and wherever they want, the story of Israel does not permit us to stray, but rather calls forth the idea of a first human in us so that we are capable of thinking about the characteristics of an primal human or god-human and thereby obtain again the original state.

According to the views of scholars the first humans were savages, a sort of ape, and have raised themselves by experiences which they have had, or inherited from their forebears, to a degree of culture which distinguishes them from beasts and stamps them as their own species. As apparent as this view is, no single basis though exists in nature for its truth. The first elephant was as docile and adroit as the current ones. The first fox had the same cunning as the foxes of our time. Throughout the animal and plant kingdoms we see perfection of the original state which will remain for all future millennia. Even if a predator may once find a new path into the henhouse, the species does not become a hair more perfect. The inventions of humanity are nothing else but such a finding of new ways for the satisfaction of their desires and needs, without thereby contributing to actual refinement. — The human steps perfect out of the hand of the creator and recognises himself and his origin; only afterwards did he begin to ponder over the latter and gave the senses too much dominance, darkening the disposition, then the knowledge was splintered and the human lost the inherited dignity in that he exchanged it for outward cleverness.

You should indeed not believe the so-called savages in Africa, America, in part also in Asia, are humans in a primal state. — Such humans living in savagery have by previous miseducation and overeducation lost the natural state and have as a result sunk down to bestiality. — The progress of humanity in its culture is only apparent, but the backwards step shows itself through the history of all ages. Where are the wise men of Greece and Israel? Where are the architects of Egypt's pyramids and temples? Where are Rome's invincible heroes? — The ceremony of all regents and peoples was to start with an image of the primal laws and depicted symbolically the powers and efficacy of them; now Asiatic and African despots have made a point of ceremony and lead nations sunken in darkness with the rod of despotism. — Even in the area of religion, this evil sometimes creeps in where priestly dominance and worldly dominance reach out their hands in order to demand the regression. — There are indeed always a few who set themselves against this regression with industry, enlightenment, and worldly philosophy; but as good as their intentions are, their striving remains just as fruitless because the tree obtains through the injection of new scions only the appearance of refinement, but in the roots it runs to seed more and more. — Knowledge of the roots, of the original state is the necessary predicate of those who want to count themselves amongst the numbers of the pure, the wise, the philosophers and Christians."

Here Mr Rückmann fell silent. — The lecture had nothing surprising for us, as instructive as it otherwise was, because the principles expressed in it agreed with the usual school views. Even the connection of the Christian religion with the story of creation, since we were in a position to consider the origin of nature and its creatures with uninhibited eyes, had lost the obscurity and mystique, and we saw in the Christian religion only the purification of a trunk whose roots spread into eternity, into God. In this sense we discussed for some time and delighted in finally having found the foundation of the Christian church in nature.

***

Discussions of the Above

When we had assembled on the deck the next day, we were extremely talkative because the lecture heard the day before had entirely covered our field, and we had already heard and read much over the various points. Amongst what was said, mainly Sigmann's words over the trinity of God stood out.

He said, "I have already often asked myself whether it was then necessary to depict God under three persons, and whether you could have not found any name which would have described all three characteristics. In this embarrassment I turned once to my dear pastor, who was horrified though by the question, and who declared in this respect any doubt and any question to be a blasphemy. I made an effort to put aside all doubts, but that did not help at all; the more I strained to believe, the stronger were my doubts. When I simply found myself in this way already in blasphemy, I endeavoured to find a more expedient name, or anyway at least an allegory. In this state I thought of an upright, sound man

100

without any professional business. He has for bourgeois society in this respect no name but that of the species man. Now he applies for a teaching position, he becomes a teacher, and gives word to his experiences and knowledge through communication. He is human and is called a teacher. His students take up his views and knowledge, radiate them back at him, and unite with him for the intended and fulfilled goal. Here there is complete unity in threefold characteristic. In my image I had human, teacher, and taught and learnt in one person. This, when applied to God, results in the name father — the power. In the name son — the efficacy of this power, the appearance of it for the activity of creation through the forming of worlds and creatures, through the animation of the human by means of the word taken from the father. Finally in the name spirit — the stepping back of the human by means of the word to the father. — Here three persons are only one in that son and spirit are contained in the father, just as above in the human the teacher and the doctrine were contained."

We thanked him for this explanation, and Grollmann expressed that he had never found the concept of the trinity of God so clearly discussed before. — We passed now to the named three pillars of the Christian church, to faith, hope, and love. Everybody knew something to say about it. Bentheim felt especially in his element and claimed that to speak about it was actually pointless, because faith, hope, and love are commanded, and we have here only to practise the duty of a positive law, without which we could not receive any Christian virtue and nor any reward promised by Christ. This dictatorship seemed to want to shake everybody, hence I took up the conversation and declared, "According to the doctrine of Mr Rückmann, blind faith and unconditional obedience are only for the weak, but the teacher, the educated man, the missionary, must raise himself to the highest possible certainty and carry proof for the necessity of the laws and their compliance at least within himself, even if he is not always capable of expressing it. Faith," I continued, "is an extremely relative power which can only express itself appropriately where we have certainty. We cannot believe something of which we are not convinced, and even if thousands of commands demand it. What we do not see, hear, and feel, we must believe.

Nobody can say with definitiveness that Alexander the Great lived, but he can believe it with definitiveness. We obtain this definitiveness of faith through concurring statements of the writers of history and through the consciousness that such an expression of power lies in the nature of the human. The necessity of a command is not to be proved by history, but rather by the agreement of it with human nature. — If faith, hope, and love are necessary for the human, then the necessity is to be investigated, and then we must believe. — The conviction of the necessity and the enlivening influence of the named characteristics never repeals the faith, to the contrary, it gives it only various gradations in that with the clarity of conviction the faith grows, with complete lack of conviction, however, it vanishes. — I believe in God because I am convinced of his existence; I put my hope in him because the power is in him, and I love him because the human cannot live without love."

As much effort as this talk also cost, my friends did not want to concur with it. A few said, "What you know, you do not need to believe." I replied to that, "Something of which we have no idea, what we cannot know and be acquainted with, we are also not in a position to believe. If we wanted to take from the human any light of knowing, you could serve up to us any knowledge." — Bentheim defended himself against my claim with every zeal. Finally Sigmann said, "The views of our friend agree completely with the remark of the apostle Paul, who also counted everything which the senses do not perceive, and which yet is and must be, under the rubric of 'faith'*." This authority calmed Bentheim, and we passed on to the three main virtues.

About the virtues, Lehnert suggested, you do not need to speak much. — Praying is necessary in that we have to ask God daily for something, be it in detail or in general. — Fasting or being moderate is a natural law in so far as it is known that immoderateness does not go with the activity of the spirit. — Giving alms, however, is a command written in our heart which needs no explanation. We all agreed with him,

---

*   [Tr.: cf. Hebrews 11:1–13. Also John 20:29.]

102

only Grollmann requested our attention for a short examination of the first virtue. —

He said, "I have already often in my life thought about the two words 'asking and praying', and could not explain to myself the difference in their meaning. I asked a learned theologian, and he answered that when we desire something from people then we ask; but when we turn with our request to God, then we pray. — I accepted this explanation without seemingly being convinced by it though. Since we have the good fortune of being taught so comprehensively by Mr Rückmann in all spiritual affairs, I could not withstand the temptation of getting enlightenment over the concepts of the named words, and have obtained the following opinion: When we desire something, be it from God or from people, we are asking. But in order to make ourselves skilled at asking God for something, we must pray. — Asking is an art. — Every art demands preparation and skill. — Draughtsmen and musicians have their special exercises (études) so that by them they can lift their performance to the highest possible degree. Prayer should accordingly be nothing more than an awakening and exercise of our spirit in order to be able to ask in the case occurring. Hence Christ also seems to say: 'You should not make many words when you want to pray.'* Praying is practice without reference or consideration to mood and content; but the request has a positive content with which the mood must be in harmony. — So much about asking and praying, with the assurance that I by this analysis think to have found only the true way of turning to God and will not be dissuaded from it anymore so easily."

We were all surprised by the novelty of this idea and thanked him for his discussion; only Bentheim was of the view that our wishes raised to God must be described with the name "prayer" and those directed at people with the designation "request or plea". Reineck responded, "If that were so, then all the characteristics of God would have to be expressed with different words than are used for people — we would not be permitted to say God's kindness, God's forbearance, etc. — I must confess that it has occurred to me as strange since

---

*   [Tr.: cf. Matthew 6:7.]

time immemorial to hear it said from one person to another, 'pray for me'. It was always to me as if one wanted to call upon the other 'learn for me!', 'walk for me!', or 'exercise yourself for me!' — The prayer is obviously, as our friend Grollmann says, a preparation, an exercise in learning to ask, and consequently it is placed in the will of the human to make himself capable for the request according to the measure of his soul's characteristics." Sigmann continued, "According to this view the usual prayerbooks are nothing more than formularies for asking, but not for praying. Certainly here the situation occurs that amongst millions of formularies just as little would one be found to be usable, as if you wanted to prescribe the petitions of the subjects to their king already in advance in one book. Of the millions of petitions written up in advance, no single one would fit for any one special case. From this it proceeds that, as we must learn to write in order to make a memorandum, we must learn to pray in order to be able to ask."

In this sense, everybody gave his bit of school wisdom to the best of his ability, for we enjoyed very much the explanations of words and concepts, and we would have continued this for even longer if Sigmann, whose earnestness did not like to linger on mere wordplay, had not brought us to the fourth point, to the foundation of the Christian church. — He gave his view, "What my friends have said up to now is good, only without the foundation we are building today and do not know whether we must tear it down again tomorrow. — The Christian religion began in Paradise with Adam. Who can give a good reason for this view? And who can justify the claim that the human possesses more insight and knowledge of God, in a word, more perfection in the original state than in the state of culture and collected experience?"

A number of answers were immediately present for the first question, in that the Messiah was already promised in Paradise. For the second question, however, nobody wanted to enter into it, as much as we had already heard about the advantages of the original state. Reineck responded, "I cannot think that the received teachings and the history of all peoples and times should not have exercised a favourable influence on the perfecting of the human race." Grollmann, who usually was adept at entering most easily into such foreign ideas, declared he could not find any connection. Lehnert alone asserted that to him this view occurred quite naturally in that he as a boy had already possessed as much cleverness as now, and he had often already in his life encountered a son teaching his father. — These claims, regardless of whether they were not so entirely unnatural, were not heeded, and it was decided to ask Mr Rückmann whether he could illuminate this subject in a specific lesson.

***

Twelfth Lesson: The Foundation of Christianity

In the evening we reported to Mr Rückmann about our investigations and doubt. — He immediately began the following lecture.

"Christianity lies before me for investigation. It is not to be reckoned what aberrations and disputes this glorious institution was already exposed to and still is. — Supernaturalists and rationalists stand on the battle ground and struggle for life and death and do not consider that their weapons, before they execute the last stroke, must disintegrate. — The supernaturalist cannot win because he abandons nature, provokes its violent powers against himself. The rationalist cannot achieve any triumph because he fences merely with words and concepts, however he does not have the courage to enter into the power of the spirit. He believes in the powers of magnets, of electricity, of galvanism, of stones and herbs; but he does not believe in any outflow of the spirit of life, in any fermenting and electrical efficacy of it. — Both are to be seen as enemies of Christianity to the extent one stimulates the other to opposition and destroys the uninhibitedness of research.

Christianity suffers just as great a dispute through the idea of an uninterrupted progress of the human species through culture and enlightenment. — Christianity strives to lead its adherents back to the origin in Paradise. Since now this runs dead straight against the usual views, you end up in doubt, dismiss with the foundations the goal and let it decay into a common moral doctrine which lacks divine origin, and which therefore makes no lasting impression on the disposition. To set aside this last dispute must therefore be our principal striving. Therefore we have to investigate what religion actually is. Whether having religion is the main aim, or whether a specific goal should be achieved by it?

Religion in the actual sense is a doctrine which occupies itself with the relationship in which humans stand towards

God, their creator, and which unites them with his spirit. —
In this idea, however, all religions are contained, those that
have already been and those that will be. — We have accordingly only to investigate which religion fulfils this aim best of
all in order to make a judgement over the worth of it.

Is religion the aim, or should such an aim be obtained
through it? That is a question which, as simple as it seems, is
not to be answered so easily. — Many think that to confess to
one religion and to fulfil its statutes is already adequate; that
which should follow will then come by itself. — If we consider
the gospels, Christ himself gives here the clearest explanation
in that he says, 'no man cometh unto the Father, but by me*.
— In my Father's house are many mansions†.' — He himself is
not the goal, but rather through him the return to the father.
Thus to the origin.

The religion is a doctrine bringing us closer to God, uniting
us with him. Christ has given the doctrine, he cannot therefore be the final goal. He teaches us to go to the father, to
which he himself led the way. — If we consider these concepts
precisely, then we cannot hover any longer in uncertainty
over the concept 'religion' and now have to investigate
whether the Christian religion corresponds to these demands.

The Christian religion shows to our souls a primitive oc-
currence of the human and thereby gives us a sign of its origin
from the father. — If the human originated from the father,
he must also return again to him, because everything that has
come into existence goes inescapably to the origin. We find
thus here for the Christian religion a distinction which no
other has, at least not with the same definitiveness. — The being of humans originated from God, the father, and will return again to him. After this I am only still lacking providing
the conviction that the human must be more perfect in his
primal state than in the educated, enlightened, and polished
one.

In the seventeenth century a philosopher spoke in a company of scholars, when the natural aptitudes of humans was
being talked about, in the following way: 'If you strike dead in

---

*　　[Tr.: John 14:6.]
†　　[Tr.: John 14:2.]

108

one day all the musicians, the song of joy and love, the most vital creator of music, would not fall silent for a minute.'

When someone reproached that view, he said furthermore, 'And if you annihilated in one day the entire human race, it would in six thousand years be again as numerous as now, with all its virtues and vices present.' — When someone also put this in doubt, he said, 'You depopulate a province which, however, has forests, meadows, ponds and streams, mountains and valleys, drive out everything in it which lives, make a wall around it so that no creature can penetrate into it, let this state last two hundred years, and you will on opening the wall find hares, deer, pigs, oxen and cows, dogs and horses, indeed every type of beast which is suited to the climate of this province. If you want to carry out the attempt still further, then you close the wall for a few more centuries, and you will also meet humans, who are far more skilful than us, reigning over the beasts and recognising themselves and nature with the unspoilt seal of human dignity.' — They objected to the philosopher that we could not have any use for such an undertaking because we would not be alive anymore. To that he responded, 'Then our offspring would, to the extent they were in fact rational enough, see the necessity of an primal state and seek it out again.' —

From this point of view we must keep in view the essential commands of the Christian church to purify ourselves of the sins of the world and to seek out the state of a newly created Adam; then we will learn to recognise the essential basis of human nature and to live according to the laws of Christianity, which has its basis in the nature of the human. — The human has, like any other creature, his natural maturity which is achieved through itself, not just through the school or in general. More precisely, the human expresses the peculiar perfection of his species just as well as in any tree the peculiarity of its own is expressed. — The human undertakes to see all of humanity as a unit and to ascribe to it a specific growth and decline, whilst all of nature argues against such an assumption. The creative power has given everything to everybody, and only to the extent you are not content with this can you think of wanting to climb still higher by the raising of the species. But just how is it thinkable to raise the whole higher, as long as you do not know your own powers, as long as you, I say, do not know yourself? — Every beast was as perfect five thousand years ago as it is now, and becomes with all the training that you seek to give this or that species in its nature not a hair more perfect. It cannot become more perfect either, because nature has made everything in the most perfect way. The beasts do not indeed have any reason, but an instinct which is infallible. — The human, if he remains true to his nature, likewise possesses for his life's goal a positive infallibility which brings him to complete maturity of spirit, and which he must possess if he should not fall behind the beasts. — The instinct of beasts refers to physical things, the instinct of humans to spiritual things. — The beast recognises bodily nourishment, the human heavenly. — Training takes from the beast its natural instinct, inappropriate training robs the human of the sight of heaven. — The horse in a natural state opens its veins itself in the event of certain illnesses; in the stables under the dominance of the whip, it loses this characteristic. In the natural state, the human recognises God and eternity without any doctrine; through the school he relinquishes this sublime gift. — Nature brings everything to the highest perfection, under the knife of culture we obtain delicate hothouse plants. — Would the oak obtain perfection in a flower pot? — A miniature plant will be grown at all events, but no tree which defies storms and bad weather. — What else surely are our theological learned institutions than such hothouse establishments where you capture the spirit of God in a school form and rob it of the ability to fly free? — In the primal state is freedom. — The primal state is the kingdom of the father to which Christ wants to lead us through his doctrine and has led the way as an example.

This is the cornerstone of the temple of Christianity, the Christian church, according to which Israel and its prophets laid the foundation, and on which Christ with his apostles, disciples, and adherents put up the Christian church. The matter certainly receives through this examination a different, more secure look in that we have to seek the kingdom of the father not in a new chaos, but rather in the nature of the human. This kingdom thereby becomes eternal and unlimited because everybody must bear in themselves the residence which was determined for them by God. The said kingdom cannot perish either, cannot be taken over by supernaturalists, nor by rationalists, because everybody who succeeds in obtaining the primal state has an inviolable property in it. By this view alone, the concept of an eternal kingdom is made complete in that it is not bound by any time or place and can be realised in all thinking and feeling beings. A summary of all teachings: the religion is the doctrine for the goal — the goal is the primal state. — In the doctrine the spirit of the primal state must be contained, just like in the primal state the nature of the doctrine."

Here Mr Rückmann fell silent. — His lecture, although of great interest, had nevertheless not caused surprise like the previous ones in that the idea of a perfect Adam and the return to his divine state had already been frequently demonstrated in dogmatic writings and sermons before. — Certainly we now saw the matter from another point of view. What previously was counsel now became the course of nature. Where we previously saw an arbitrary intervention of the will of God, we now recognised the necessary activity of a power of creation which had to express itself according to irrevocable laws, just as it was expressed. — If we usually placed the kingdom of the father in invisible regions of the universe and could not imagine it at all, we now saw ourselves already in it and needed just to make ourselves skilled in learning to feel and recognise all the blessings which it conferred. — We thanked Mr Rückmann with sincere hearts for his lecture and left with the assurance of reinforcing in ourselves what we had heard as much as possible.

***

Self-Discussion of What was Heard

The next morning we came together soon on the deck and expressed our views over the necessity and perfection of the primal state. As natural and irrefutable as the return to it had seemed as long as Mr Rückmann was speaking, the conviction was already weaker once we found ourselves alone. Grollmann, morose over the unreliability of our powers of spirit, said, "The human is a true change machine. At one moment carried away by something, he does not know for the other thing anymore what had enthused him. The perfection of a primal state was so clear to me yesterday that I had believed there could be no doubt over it anymore. Today my life story tells me that I listened from my youth on to nothing else but to take care of the ennoblement of humanity through learnedness, invention, and industry. Should then all the experiences made be of no use? — Should everything which we learnt from others and have produced ourselves, instead of bringing us closer to the goal, have distanced us from it? — Free me of this doubt, otherwise I must renounce my calling and publicly confess that I am no Christian."

Sigmann, who was seldom accustomed to expressing a special sympathy by mien or gestures, had at the end of this talk caught the speaker sharply in the eye, and we were expectant as to the reply which he, to all appearances, was resolved to give. He did not ponder for long either and spoke with a solemn earnestness.

"What our friend expressed to us is good. He has lead us to the cliff face which we have to climb up if we ever want to arrive in the region of a contented certainty. — The cornerstone of the Christian church is the perfection of the human in the primal state. If this perfection is true, and the human can achieve without school or training his complete maturity, then the nature of the Christian religion rests on irrevocable laws of life; but if the primal state is the childhood of humanity, then our church stands on loose sand and is exposed to downfall with every storm. The either-or is sharply drawn, and we know now that it must be our chief business to straighten out the original characteristics of human nature."

Bentheim was during these talks quite uneasy, he took up the conversation and said, "What our two friends have said is according to the ways of men solid and good. The either-or which they drew with sharp lines enlightens us about the nature of the Christian religion — it wants to be believed and therefore logic must fall silent before it. Only through the power of faith can Christ become alive in us, as we are taught by the church fathers, as Christ himself taught when he said, 'blessed are they that have not seen, and yet have believed.'*"

Biblical texts exercise on us who were educated in a strictly Christian way constantly an almost absolute force, and therefore none of the previous speakers trusted themselves to say something about this, and we were already resolved to separate without further debate when Reineck held us back, and said, "We are and remain timid schoolboys, and even if you brought the truth down from heaven to us. Mr Rückmann does everything to release any authority around us and to liberate us, and we tremble backwards before a text without having the courage to investigate whether what was said before is to be combined with it. I say that a faith which has to be afraid of reason must stand on weak legs. I believe as firmly as anyone in the truth of the Bible and put forward therefore against faith the principle that a reason which is not yet in a position to comprehend the truth of the Bible is still seeking with blindfolded eyes and must await the light which only serious research will give."

We accorded these words united applause and decided to begin the research immediately and seek out the trail which could lead us to conviction of the perfection of the primal state. Everybody endeavoured to say something conclusive in this respect, but again and again we failed on the idea imbibed since youth of an uninterrupted progress of the human race, a propaganda which our species must someday rise to heaven in order to become not only like God, but finally God himself. I requested attention for a few words which I wished to say, and said, "If somewhere in this respect enlightenment should be found, then it can only occur in the story. It lies before us and shows us in Adam an original son. The question of whether he is the progenitor of the human race does not come into consideration here because it is with our investigation not to do with the first of all humans, but rather with one originating from God. Adam was a human produced by God and birthed by nature. Was he more perfect than us? According to the Bible story, he had the word of God in himself and spoke with God like we speak with our fathers. He sinned, and the

---

*   [Tr.: John 20:29.]

word seemed to have darkened in him; only he still stood there as the progenitor of a people which became as numerous as the sand in the sea*. No laws or state institutions were to be seen in those days because the human in his primal state had as little need of a law as the deer in the forest, and he carried the plan of his life within himself. — This certainly sounds to our ears, which are encircled and entwined by laws, so alien and strange that we almost cannot grasp it at all. If the residents of a forest and the birds in the air did not show us the possibility of a positively independent free life, we would consider it an absurdity; but thus the matter stands before us, and we have only to inquire to what extent the human can be free or not.

In the history of the world there is found, outside the Bible, several more traces of a first-born state. The dynasty of the Chinese ruler originates from heaven. The progenitor of it is a son of Fu. The first constitutions of the land were, like the laws of Israel, given by god, and if something can testify to the perfection of a primal state, then it is this, that China boasts of the duration of its legal constitution being eight thousand years, whereas the most policed empires of later history existed not even half as long and often with the greatest exertions of worldly cleverness collapsed in a few centuries, or at least had to take on an entirely different form. Romulus is according to what history tells us a son of man created from the primal power, nourished by wolves, and without possessing a stick of property laid the germ for an empire which lasted over twelve hundred years and prescribed the world's laws. Cyrus, raised as a shepherd, reigned over a large part of Asia. All dynasties of that part of the world derived their origin from a primitive man. Even in America, they have found races who will have received their origin from the sun; — Teut is a son of Sol and Hertha, and the traditions call him the son of the perfect power. — According to all these indications, I think, we should possess a thread which gets us closer to knowing the state of human primal nature. If we fully consider history and contemplate that the earlier races were closer to their primitive forebears than we are, then I ask, are

---

*   [Tr.: cf. Genesis 32:12.]

we more rational, magnanimous, and artistic than our ancestors? — To the extent we take into consideration the names of a Socrates, Plato, Zoroaster, Confucius, Pythagoras, Euclid, and many others, we must confess that they, even if under different forms, thought just as deeply as our foremost scholars. When we look at the areas of art whose epochs are not so familiar to me, but of which I know though as much as that the Greeks must have reached a height which our current artists still look up to in astonishment. If we finally apply the principle found above to be true to our task, we can conclude that the times when the human form showed itself at its most cultured and powerful must have also been the most perfect states. When we just in this respect toss a glance at our forebears, the Germans, and compare them with us, I think the result cannot be uncertain. The usual measure of the man was seven feet — their power was gigantic — their stamina like steel and iron. But when we then look at their moral development, we must be astonished over the simple manner of their veneration of God, over their loyalty and probity, over virtues and moral characteristics which sound to us now like folk tales. Those sons of nature did not need any messiah, they received directly from the eternal primal light of the father, their Allfather, their spiritual needs and lived already in the here and now in Valhalla. After these observations, I am so animatedly convinced of the perfection of the primal state that I only regret seeing myself so distant from it, and having almost no hope of being able to ever attain it."

My friends had listened to this talk with great attention and expressed their undivided satisfaction over it. Sigmann said I could after this attempt replace Mr Rückmann for him in an emergency. Even Bentheim, although much seemed not so entirely faithful to the Bible, expressed his agreement. Lehnert, perhaps the most natural of us all, also expressed his view, and said, "From youth on I have heard speak of nothing else but education of the people, the spread of enlightenment, and the benefit of new inventions in all realms of the arts and sciences, and if you wanted to enthuse me for a virtue, you showed me an example which made this or that possible. Now I am at once taught that the human does not need all of that because he can arrive at the goal through himself. I must confess, to start with it seems impossible to find one's way in such extremes. But now I feel that it would be more natural if the human could obtain everything, like the other creatures, from his own power, as it were from a sort of higher instinct."

Still more was spoken in this sense; but strangely, the more uninhibitedly everyone expressed themselves, the clearer it became to us that a hindrance to entirely securing our conviction still prevailed; for, as we considered the world, it was clear that there no standstill is possible in that the spirit of the times constantly tore down today what it constructed yesterday, and from this change constantly new and better things seem to come forth. Since we were absolutely incapable of untying these knots, we decided to reveal to Mr Rückmann our embarrassment and to ask him to obtain light for us.

***

Thirteenth Lesson: The Three Kingdoms

We arrived that evening at the designated time at Mr Rückmann's. Hardly had we enjoyed some food, than we presented to him the results of our discussions and our inability to obtain a secure view over the necessity of an advancing culture and of the constancy of the primal state. He had barely heard our wishes, when he began as follows.

"I drew with a few contours yesterday the perfection of the natural state. As infallibly as such a state exists, we see though in the course of creation a sort of falling and rising which can easily confuse us in our inquiries in that certain kingdoms pass over from one into the other without showing a definite boundary. The mineral and plant kingdoms are so closely connected that the observer often does not know in which class this or that is to be counted. The corals are half plant and half animal. To the most thorough naturalist still more such phenomena must be known. — The Egyptians, who contemplated nature the sharpest of all, drew in this respect a hieroglyph which was a depiction that was half animal and half plant, and added the sensible explanation that the plant with increasing tending of the ground suppresses and devours the animal, but with the reversed process, where the animal is well nourished, but the plants are neglected, the former takes the victory, the plant either pulls from the ground and animates, or it pushes from itself and begins its life course as an animal freed from the earth. Those deep-thinking researchers showed yet another image, in which we see the human as a heavenly creature and at the same time as an animal. — Between the animal kingdom and residents of the other side stands the human half as animal and half as angel. If the animal becomes well cared for, then it swallows the angel; but nourish the human with fruits of the spirit and of heaven, and the angel vanquishes the animal, and the human enters into the temple of light. — There is no image in all of nature which describes the standpoint of the human more clearly; there is, however, also none from which all the aberrations in which humanity has fallen and will yet fall are more certainly to be derived. — The human stands between earth and heaven. Creature and spirit are the poles. Both attract one another, or repel themselves according to their direction. — This direction shall be given through understanding and reason, and if these allow themselves to be seduced, by knowledge. The human has sufficient means of assistance and can therefore not lack to the extent he strives to use them appropriately and keeps creature and spirit in appropriate balance.

The kingdom of senses and the kingdom of spirit are given by nature and by God, and are not to be altered and modelled. Nobody can tell the throat vinegar shall taste sweet and sugar sour. All the characteristics of the senses are so positively given that no class, no culture, no age, no climate, and no school could change anything about them. — Here there is accordingly stability on which the wit of propaganda falls down. Like the kingdom of senses, so too is the kingdom of the spirit in its own positive power which acts the same in both the beggar and the millionaire. — The poor mother loves her child as tenderly as the rich one. The former like the latter turns with the illnesses of her loved ones to one and the same power. The entire difference here lies in the receptivity of the disposition which through previous stimuli reveals itself more or less distinctly. — The feeling of an eternal life, the wish of a future continuation, a continuation without pain and worry, without suppression and persecution, are written in the hearts of all earthlings and come alive as soon as we express them just once. — Even the essential features of all sciences lie in the spirit of anyone, and the good judge of character finds among uneducated country people often the results of a reflection which would shame the most practised schoolman. — All knowledge is a sort of inspiration. This inspiration is of a twofold sort: either we receive from others, or from nature, and in it the living spirit of all knowledge, of which every human child has a breath, imparts to us what we need. This kingdom is also stable, and nothing is to be taken from it, nor added, and where propaganda has the audacity to assert its progress here, it works destructively, and instead of the hoped-for fruits it germinates poverty and confusion of the spirit.

It is certainly difficult to speak comprehensibly about this, because one has departed far too far from the matter; but so much must be said, that humanity without such an inspiration of the spirit would possess neither learnedness, science, nor art. Who teaches the human in all the affairs of life? Necessity. — To collect sustenance, to defend yourself and your own, to love, to raise, and to recommend them to an eternal power are things the resident of the forest understands just as well as, and often even better than the most educated townspeople. Such a one possesses courage, magnanimity, and resignation which, if we were to witness it, would have to shame us. And if these characteristics are not those which actually constitute the human, without which he remains under all circumstances only a half-creature and could not place himself under the class of free beings? The animals in the forest are free, the birds of the air are free, only the human is wrapped in bonds. — The animals of the forest and the birds of the air take pleasure in unspoilt mood in their existence, but the human also feels with the most joyful events of his life the press of the chains in which he beats himself. Where do these bonds come from? Where do these chains come from? Has nature — has God given them? No! — The divine in the human is free, and the creaturely is! — But between these two, reason, that selfish guard, has placed itself and plucks the fruits from the tree of free spiritual knowledge, criticises and presses them for so long until their pure juice evaporates and nothing is left behind but an arrogant critique by which the human raises himself above the spirit and thinks to know better than everyone. Just as they proceed in the kingdom of the senses, and since they cannot weaken or suppress the activity of them, they raise such to a degree that, because of self-preservation, it becomes necessary to rein them in and bring in legal limits. This neglect of the spirit and artificial stimulation of the senses are the basis of a new kingdom which was erected not by God and nature, but rather by humans.

The human lives in two primal kingdoms — in the kingdom of the senses and in the kingdom of the spirit. — In these two he is placed by God, and he has made a third himself, and that is the world. — In the entourage of mind, acumen, wit, cleverness, shrewdness, ambition, thirst for power, art, sciences, wealth, poverty, agriculture, industry of all sorts, streets, ships, tolls, institutes, universities, armies, state institutions, churches, palaces, preachers, teachers, world improvers, humanists, cosmopolitans, rigourists, fatalists, pietists, nationalists, materialists, etc., reason founded a kingdom, and made such institutions so that the end is not to be foreseen. — It is the kingdom which like the retiring ocean flows thence and carries away everything with it. It is the tower of Babel where you hope to climb to heaven and continue building for evermore, but never come to an end — where you explain what happens in one century in the next to be inexpedient and to tear it down. — This is the kingdom where there is no standstill and no rest, where you remain in the whirl of a constant progress always in the same place, but are ruled by the illusion that humanity is destined for an uninterrupted striding forward, and the individual only has value in so far as he also intervenes in the whole tearing down and building up again. This is the kingdom of the beast in Revelations. — It is the kingdom of giants, the inviolable power whose signs and names everybody who is born must carry if he wants to have any worth and existence in it. — Thus we live in a kingdom made by humanity itself and do not surmise that, the more we render homage to it, the further we are removed from the primal state of our nature. — We live in the kingdom of a grandeur whose brilliance blinds us, which is seemingly infinite because we do not see its limits, where you hope to achieve everything because art and nature are connected, a kingdom of the highest perfection, indeed, according to the views of the wise men of the world, to bring about the kingdom of God. — Unfortunately this is all just appearance and shimmer which deceives humans, but which brings them not to perfection, to primal nature, to maturity. — In this great kingdom no independence, no stop, and no spiritual freedom are thinkable, because here no standstill, no rest may reign. — In the kingdom of the world, one drives the other. — Standstill would be regression, because here the elements can only be kept pure and remain active in constant motion.

Three kingdoms make demands on the human; to which does he belong? — Firstly the kingdom of the senses, for he grows up in it; that of the world in so far as he becomes a citizen of it; then the kingdom of the spirit because he shall emerge from it and return again to it.

The *kingdom of the senses* stands irrevocable in that the first human had the same senses which our descendants will have thousands of years from now. The *world* is the kingdom of propaganda and leads with all reason constantly from one confusion to the next. — The *spirit* is a pure product of eternity and was and will always remain the same. Worldly cleverness can misjudge and deny it, but that is directly as much as if the blind man denied the light of the sun. The kingdom of the senses, just like the kingdom of the spirit, is without sin, but the world is full of horrors. — As soon as the man of the world passes over to the kingdom of the senses, he transfers his pride, his fury, and his passions into it and becomes worse than the most terrible beast, becomes in a word a creature of hell because hell, just like heaven, also resides in his heart.

The three kingdoms are: darkness, the world, and light. Darkness is of the primal beginning, just as light is — between light and darkness the human has built his own kingdom, the world, and merges in it light and darkness together in such a way that you seldom know whether you are serving the light or the darkness. — The world pays homage with the same pomp to the overgilded idols of the night as to the images of light finished with tinsel. The world celebrates no primal nature, but rather self carved gods, and even if they may still speak so much of the unity of God, they nevertheless pay homage to all the imaginary divinities of the day, place here a poet, there a juggler, here an actor, there a singer, here a hero, there a diplomat, then again a fanatic, and finally an incomprehensible scholar on the altar for their adoration and think the eternal light will delight enormously over seeing its million steps removed reflection admired here. — There is only one, and this is the spirit. — There is only one spirit, and this is God. Anyone who seeks this spirit finds God; but anyone who does not strive to recognise him in his complete clarity distances himself again and again from him and finally comes to an end in the darkness.

The senses need no doctrine; they exercise their rights without any impulse. The spirit needs no doctrine — just as the eagle seeks the highest mountain peaks for its residence, so too does the spirit strive up towards heaven. Anyone who holds the eagle in the depths cripples it and takes from it the centrifugal force of its regal flight. Anyone who entwines the spirit with the bonds of the world robs it of the freedom of independent knowing and doing and drags it into the dust. Render therefore unto Caesar the things which are Caesar's; and unto God the things that are God's*. — Give to the world what is of the world, and to heaven what is of heaven, then your soul will save itself. The world is to it a sojourn for being tested, where it can show whether it is serious about belonging to heaven and being privy to its blessings. — The three kingdoms are hell, the world, and the kingdom of heaven. Hell throws its slaves into the darkness and places the fire of fury in their souls for self-torment. The world drives and chases its venerators for as long as until the life force vanishes and death clears the field. The kingdom of heaven! What do you give your sons? — Freedom and love. — Can there be aside from these anything else worth wishing? Can a being desire more than unlimited freedom and the feeling of love? No! With these the temple of the highest happiness is completed, and seven and seventy times will those lament† who do not have the power to strive for such a state and to sacrifice the world's caprices and vanities for it.

The creation is complete, the paths are open, therefore we want to finish for today and see tomorrow in which of these three kingdoms Christ revealed his life course and spread his light. Anyone who knows the gospels only to some extent will not be in doubt for long about it; only, the extent to which the appearance of that sublime mediator agrees with what has been expressed up to now, or does not, is worth the most thorough investigation because we thereby obtain a firm

---

*   [Tr.: Matthew 22:21.]
†   [Tr.: cf. Genesis 4:24.]

standpoint and place ourselves above all the doubt and hair-splitting of today's theologians."

Here he fell silent. — We felt extremely pleased about the day's lecture and expressed it openly. Reineck declared that it was for him as though a stone had been taken from his heart by the day's instruction. The stability of the primal state could so little be denied as the particularity of an oak. According to the division into the three named kingdoms, the human is called to progress, just as for stability, and you do not need any law at all but that of giving to each what belongs to each.

Everybody expressed themselves in this sense. Mr Rückmann took pleasure in our quickness to learn and called upon us to think about the matter carefully in order to find a secure basis for the Christian church which we would build up in the next gathering.

***

The Zeitgeist Lurks

When we came together the next morning, the previous day's mood had fallen significantly; not as if we were putting in doubt Rückmann's views, but rather because the depiction of his three kingdoms made us take a look at ourselves, which was nothing less than to our advantage. Grossman, after he perceived our mood, said, "I have looked around in the three kingdoms and cannot work out where I find myself. I have previously remained free of raw sensuality, but that was perhaps more owing to the supervision of others than to my free will. Indeed I like to gaze, listen, and play, only this appears to lie in the nature of those senses which are without sin. The kingdom of the spirit, the primal nature of the human, I do not yet know them in myself, and I fear to have lost them irretrievably, notwithstanding that I surmise their perfection. But, what shall I say about the kingdom of the world? This has, although I find myself at sea, cut off from it as it were, embraced me entirely. I feel too clearly that, if I had received my father's wealth, I would not now be journeying to India as a missionary, but consuming my money in comfort. I also feel that, to the extent fate smiles on me and should provide me appropriate sustenance, I will not hold the laborious pilgrim's staff for long, but would like rather to choose a more leisurely life; therefore I am living, although by appearance separated from it, entirely of the world, and cannot be considered a model of a free, spiritual primal human for those I baptise in the future."

This unreserved confession made a deep impression on everyone. Lehnert said that if he could have done what he wanted, he would have become a pharmacist. Sigmann declared his life's highest wish had consisted of one day becoming a teacher of mathematics, and he would yet take up this path now if a prospect offered itself to do so. Everybody confessed their favoured prospects and the sadness of knowing themselves shut off from them. After everybody had expressed themselves in this way and an unusual melancholy had spread amongst us, I took up the conversation and said, "My friends! Even if everything which we dreamed of in youth may be lost to us, we must consider that we have found a signpost which shows us the correct path of life. The world has won our fantasies for itself, but a kindly fate has preserved our personalities from its snares. We are free of its bonds, are free of the thousands of temptations to which one is exposed in it. Our life course requires already of us that we give ourselves over to the kingdom of the spirit with all our powers, if we do not want to stumble on it and, instead of sowing flowers, sowing thorns. — Render therefore unto Caesar, the world, the things which are Caesar's and the world's; and unto God the things that are God's. We can give nothing to the world, all the more though to the spirit. If the world wants to reward us for our efforts, then we would be foolish to not want to accept it, because then we could always yet consider what we owe it, and what we owe God. I will continue to wander on my life course happily and want to have no other wish than to be a worthy servant of our sublime religion whose spirit, when it is for our best, can also provide the richest reward in the world."

This address gave the others courage again and they gave each other their word to keep their eye on the set goal and to not pay attention to the apparitions of the world spirit.

***

Fourteenth Lesson: Christ Comes into the World

Hardly had we informed Mr Rückmann the next day of the apparitions of the world spirit, than he gave us the following thoughts.

"The human has divided himself into three kingdoms — into hell, the world, and the kingdom of heaven. Into which of these kingdoms could Christ surely come? Into hell? This did not desire him. Into the kingdom of heaven? This did not need him. Into the world! — since it was where his light could still have an effect. He made it his task to show misled humanity the right way out of its labyrinthian corridors, and fulfilled it in a way like nobody had previously done and which will hardly occur after him. — In the most perfect primal state he withstood the challenges of hell and the world, remained pure from the dogmas and shimmering theorems of the priests and scholars, and gave the world through word and deed the example that it is possible in the spirit of the father, that is in the primal law, to live, to speak, and to act.

The gospels have indeed been challenged by newer theologians and scholars in a way that the less powerful could easily be tempted to think the entire matter were only an arbitrary compilation of fantasies of easily tempted weaklings or ambitious fanatics; it is therefore necessary above all to consider and reinforce the truth of the gospels and their value.

If we judge the gospels to be a merely literary work, then we must say that it already takes first place in this respect. Must it be simply asked to this end, what is the highest aim of literature? — The highest aim of it is to make us familiar and conversant with spiritual truths; that work which fulfils this most completely deserves therefore the first place. For the stated goal, literature possesses two means: either the cold, calm doctrine, or poetry. — The doctrine is suited to the practised thinker, the scholar, for everyone else it is a tree without fruit. — The disposition of those who do not occupy themselves with learnedness demands poetry which stirs the heart in pictures and teaches the human the truth with the help of feelings. — Where the truth shows itself in pictures, there is poetry. — Where the picture leads to truth, it passes over into our disposition, and every life force is awoken and illuminated by it. Now it is to be asked whether the gospels fulfil their goal according to this view.

As poetic work, the New Testament of the Bible is the first book of humanity. — We have no other that is to be compared with it. — Homer's Iliad, that giant work which the poets of all later centuries and our time look up to like children, delivers high ideals of heroic virtues, but no single one in which the spiritual characteristics of human nature express themselves as completely. Ulysses had to cross lands and seas and finally had to have the path to hell shown to him in order to hear spiritual truths. — Virgil's Aeneid is a classic book, but how far does the hero of it stand back from the ideal which the Bible establishes? — When we consider the works of the great geniuses of more recent history, a Milton, Dante, Shakespeare, Schiller, Goethe, then we cannot hold back our admiration; but how much are their images lacking for such a pure primal state in which we see Christ? For the educated, for the scholars and artists, the gospels are, even without historical reference, of such high value that they should use them properly for the study of their philosophical purification and artistic education. — But if they still possess historical reality, then we obtain the living image of a human dignity before which we can do nothing else but stand with deep veneration and feel driven to resemble it at least in a few parts*. We want therefore to also consider the history of this sublime master and see whether we do not find a few documents for its truth.

The Christian religion exists, consequently it must have had a founder. — Everything great and glorious which exercises an influence on humanity emanates from a single indi-

---

* The revilers of the sublimeness of Christ say the writers of his history were raw and uneducated people. Joseph II, Frederick the Great, and Napoleon have lived in our enlightened and educated times, and nevertheless they have despite multiple attempts found no writers of history who would be in a position to draw them suitably, and to hold up such a successful portrait as we have in Christ. — Oh Pharisees! — Oh scholars! —

vidual. — All philosophical systems have their first founder. — All religions stem from a single founder. — Without the energy of such heroic spirits their doctrine would have not come to life anywhere. — Had Luther been frightened off on his way to Worms, then the Reformation, despite all his writings, would have remained undone. He had to reaffirm his decision to sacrifice himself for the matter, through that it obtained significance and following. Had Christ after the appointment of the supper, instead of handing himself over to his tormenters, almost by himself, had escaped to foreign lands, then Christianity would, with all its doctrines and texts, not have been able to strike root. He had to set the seal on his word with his death, through that it received value and significance, and still continues to live in the dispositions of every adherent. — Denying the truth of the person of Christ means just as much as plucking fruit from a tree and yet claiming there is no fruit tree. — The doubt, however, over the historical truth of Christ has not yet caused so much evil as the doubt in the truth of the doctrine expressed by him. We want therefore to seek to illuminate this point to some extent.

Christ teaches rebirth in the spirit, resurrection from death, and ascension to heaven. — It is already these three points which do not want to become clear to human reason and therefore are frequently challenged. — You ask along with Nicodemus[*], how can the human be born again? — Everything which is there is produced by the father and should return through the purest, the most sacred, should return through the human to the origin. Hence Christ says, through me to the father[†]; and so everybody will be able to speak who has become a genuine Christian. — But, in order to give the matter in more detail, we must still consider humanity in its origin.

We have already seen above that the human, produced on earth by the spirit of God, has arisen through a multiple purification and fermentation from the plant world, and had his head directed to heaven. In this erect stance the limbs separate from his body in complete agreement from one another,

---

[*]   [Tr.: cf. John 3:4.]
[†]   [Tr.: cf. John 14:6.]

meanwhile remaining nonetheless in the closest way connected to a whole. The spirit fermented into the finest spreads through all the stages in separate yet connected circumstances and gives them the ability to act on one another and produce a wealth of life which would not be produced in a stooped posture. — These stage-circumstances are felt by the human to start with only in his outer organs; but as he looks and feels within himself, the inner organs too, according to the relationship of their place and position, come to life, and the rebirth is achieved.

You should indeed not think as if the rebirth were something opposite to our corporeal nature, no, it is based on the form and the construction of our body, and anyone who has never felt the effectiveness of his inner organs is like a house owner who has lost the key to the entrance to his property. Within is the life, within the core, outside are the suckling branches for nourishing the inner-being and preserving it in action.

Every organ of the human body has a double activity, a creaturely and a spiritual. — The eye sees the objects, but also distinguishes them and counts them. — The ear hears sounds, but also hears the notes of music. It perceives bangs, noise, and notes, but also hears at the same time the words of language in its inexhaustible flexibility and culture, in its grace and instruction, in all its turnings and colours which delight, instruct, and make us ripe for heaven. — If we investigate the mouth, which is skilled at various tasks, both physical and spiritual, we must marvel over the mix of diversity with such simplicity. — Does it not now mean to judge against all order if you claim the inner organs are mere servants of a material mechanism, are mere lumps of flesh or dead bones for nourishing the body or carrying it around? Does not the heart already give clear evidence that the inner organs are just as capable, indeed still more so, of a spiritual activity? — The lungs, the liver, the kidneys, the heart, the intestines, etc., everything is full of the spirit, and anyone who does not recognise this is not yet living, and even if he would yet know so much; but anyone who feels the spiritual activity of the inner organs has entered his house, is reborn in the spirit and will recognise his destiny without any doctrine from without.

Formerly the human had no other school than his inner life. With the school from without, the inner seemed to have become superfluous, and humanity lost itself in a self-made shimmer. Now it must return to its original property and not directly renounce the outer school, but subordinate it to the inner eternal laws and thereby obtain again the human dignity lent by God and nature.

The resurrection from death is a puzzle to many, and the rationalist bristles against this command like the sanctimonious Buddhist priest against a natural freedom of the spirit. — The human must rise up from the dead; he must thus die. — But here the talk is not of the natural death, but rather of that which the perverse human suffers, and from which he must rise up. — The world has girded us with a new human, indeed made us into a new human who, far from the primal state and the kingdom of the father, does not know his high destiny anymore. — This worldly human must die and arise purified.

Many want to deny the necessity of this death and to claim the once innate characteristics will develop and purify by themselves with the creaturely death. — This, however, means as much as to say you wanted to claim a tree only bears good fruit when it has decayed. — Just why are humans so clever in all other things, and in respect to themselves, to their self-awareness, so limited? — When we take an arrogant man or a miser who only lives his passion, if all the feelings of his heavenly nature are not stripped from him, can he achieve his innate dignity no other way than through the death of the miser or the arrogant man? — This you will indeed like to admit, but the resurrection has turned into a hypothesis.

The resurrection is just as necessary as death. — Or do you believe the miser has still other powers in himself than those which he put into operation for his passion? — No, he has no other powers; everything which he possesses, he has sacrificed to his passion and he must now purify this, baptise it, and make it suitable for higher activity, then he has arisen from the dead and can in the feeling of his reawakened life nourish himself with the powers of heaven and achieve his perfection.

After the resurrection, the ascension to heaven can follow. — At first glance you would think that it *must* take place after the resurrection. But even here nature goes its inexorable way. When the human decides in everyday life to learn an art, science, or a business, he has torn himself away from the uncertainty in which he previously found himself, and now turns to a specific way of life. But he is not yet what he intends to become — diligence and zeal to learn thoroughly that which he has grasped, penetration into the spirit of it is necessary, and to inquire for as long as until he overcomes the school and can establish himself as a master who bears the thing within himself. — Thus the one arisen from the dead must endeavour to make his nature ripe for the ascension so that he knows the matter not only according to the words, but according to the feeling and the nature of it, then he travels, with the throwing away of the last shackles of doctrine and constraint, towards heaven and is enthroned there in undisputed, infallible glory as a free being in the radiance of the father.

After these thoughts it will hardly be necessary to say to where Christ came, indeed to where he must have come. — He came into the kingdom of the world, not in order to destroy it, but rather to obtain it for the kingdom of heaven. He came into the world when its dominion had achieved an extent and generality like never before. — Rome's eagles were already distributed over three continents. The religious laws of this giant state bore the stamp of world domination. The primal laws of Israel had sunk down into ceremonial service, and the priestly class formed nothing more than an innate caste in the state constitution, and paid homage to the world as well as the state servants and scribes. — Under such circumstances Christ entered the world, established himself as an uncorrupted man of God, and gave his contemporaries a model of intimacy with God and of the possibility of being able to unite again with the primal power.

All teachers of religion before Christ indeed also came into the world as fighters for the primal law, but for most of them this was the kingdom of the eternal darkness; they wanted to overcome hell in the world or the world as hell, and hence their adherents had to separate themselves from everything which the world offered them, in so far as the world as hell conflicted entirely with the kingdom of heaven. — We see in this respect the Indian penitents, the inviolability of the Brahmans, the Egyptian priests , the severity of the Israelites, and many other peoples. — Christ was the first who recognised the world as a creation of humanity and saw the necessity of having the world and the kingdom of heaven exist next to one another and of fostering one through the other. — On this basis the Christian religion is the most beneficial of all, because it sanctifies relations of states and the bourgeois order, but without losing from view for even a moment its final goal, obtaining the citizens of the kingdom of heaven. — Render therefore unto Caesar the things which are Caesar's; and unto God the things that are God's!* — With this command Christ gave the instruction on how the human has to live in order to comply with his teachings. We live among humans, in the world; children of the world are our neighbours and relatives whom we, according to the Christian laws, must love as thyself†. — Be subject to the bourgeois order and love God over everything, those are the two essential laws of Christianity, and already on this basis its spread must be just as welcome to the regents and state officials as to the subjects.

From this little thing you will already see what philosophical depth and what poetic teachings Christianity contains within itself, and what a boon it is to support and spread it as much as possible; but also how daring and wicked it is to impugn any of its pillars or principles; because with the removal of any single one the entire edifice can collapse."

Mr Rückmann fell silent. — His lecture, irregardless of each of us being convinced of the reliability of the Biblical truths, had the effect that we thought only this evening we had become true Christians. We expressed our thanks over it openly and left with the assurance of impressing his lessons deep into our hearts.

***

---

*   [Tr.: Matthew 22:21.]

†   [Tr.: cf. Leviticus 19:18, Matthew 22:39, Mark 12:31, Romans 13:10, and 1 John 4:11.]

Self-Examination

When we had assembled the next morning, everybody wanted to express his views over what had been heard the day before first. — Sigmann, however, requested our attention and said, "In order to adequately test such important things as we heard yesterday, they must be considered in appropriate order and hierarchy. — I have drawn up the course of yesterday's lecture and request that my friends take it as a guide for their discussion so as to not confound one thing with another and confuse ourselves. The main points were the following:

1) The worth of the gospels as literary work.
2) The truth of the person of Christ.
3) His doctrine of rebirth, resurrection from the dead, and ascension to heaven.
4) Christ did not come into hell and not into heaven, but into the world.

When our friends want to speak, then I consider it expedient to keep to this order and to base our judgements accordingly."

Grollmann asked to speak to this and said, "I would not have had the courage in all my life to put the gospels in the class of literary phenomena had Mr Rückmann not brought me to it; and yet I see how important it is to allocate to a fitting place a book which is given to us as a guide to life. The image of Christ is the most beautiful and most sublime which ever flowed from the hand of an artist. How imperfect are the images of the greatest poets in comparison? How mean and almost featureless the descriptions in the Oriental tales of a thousand and one nights? — Indeed, how incomplete are the edifices of all the familiar philosophers who have for the scholars a barely visible value, for the uneducated none at all. How gloriously by contrast does the Bible connect humans with God, the creature with the spirit, the age with eternity, and the world with heaven! — If I now take fully into consideration that the drawn up image of Christ is not only an ideal, but rather a portrait, then I must confess that humanity, in possession of such a work, should be protected from all confusion and never end up in doubt and uncertainty again. I will learn the gospels by heart and am convinced of obtaining more thereby than the schools of all universities could give me.

Bentheim, to whom the conditional doubt in the existence of Christ was already an infringement on the essence of the Christian teachings, replied to this talk, "What our friend Grollmann has said is good and fruitful for doubting dispositions. It is admittedly of great value to consider the Bible as the first book of literature, because through that the vain man of the world receives a spur to appreciate it better, to the extent that such a one must be drawn by external lustre. Only, the Bible, and especially the gospels, are not only a work of art, but rather of truth. Christ lived and acted, of that everybody must be convinced who is not entirely blinded. Certainly it is difficult to give proof to the unbelieving, because they find a thousand ways of glossing over their errors, and I must confess that I was sometimes in great difficulties over this point. History is not clear and consistent enough in this respect; the philosophical evidence is contradicted by pretexts, and so you see yourself often required, equipped with the best weapons, to withdraw again without having inflicted a wound on the enemy. — The evidence of Mr Rückmann, however, is of the sort that anyone who is not entirely obdurate must feel battered. It also confirms here the experience that we do not know how to see most truths and how to establish them, because they lie to close to us. Christianity is, thus there was a Christ. — Lutheranism exists, thus there was a Luther. — The Kantian philosophy is present, thus a Kant lived. — Schiller, Goethe, Klopstock, Herder, Cicero, Julius Caesar, Virgil, Homer, and others existed, for their works attest to them. — Christ existed, Christianity testifies for him. He himself indeed did not document himself in writing, but others did it, and hence the description of him is a portrait from life, and even if imperfections should be in this portrait, we must take into consideration that no artist is in a position to give a complete copy of an original; their work always lags behind the latter. — Indeed the enemies of Christ have yet another reproach against the truth of his existence in that they claim the gospels are a mere fabrication. — Here I feel forced to bring my warmest thanks to our fatherly teacher that he put me in a position to also speak about this with certainty. — If the image of the gospels is a portrait, then the matter has its complete reality; but if it is a fabrication, a product of the poetic arts, then the writer must have been at a standpoint where he not only bore the ideal within himself, but realised it. — Be it therefore as it may, the person of Christ is confirmed in a way that it betrays the deepest darkness to impugn it in that either the writer or the drawn image always satisfies our expectations. This last phrase should indeed not be a proof of the weakness of my faith, but rather only a weapon against the obstinate ones who think to have destroyed the Bible with the rejection of the personhood of Christ. — Christ lived, he wandered amongst humanity, for no poetic talent would be in a position to give such a glorious, perfect, divine portrait without having an original."

"Bravo!", we all cried out. — Sigmann said, "My friend Bentheim has exceeded himself in that he, so severely devout, had the courage to work out fully the comparison between original and portrait. And he is perfectly correct — in order to describe a great man, you must yourself possess greatness. Had Napoleon not lived, nobody would have been able to sketch an historical image of him without a Napoleon himself having been. — Indeed, despite that, that he lived among us, at least among our parents, nobody has yet been found who can portray him in the way the apostles drew their master. On this basis the reproach of the gospels being mere fabrications loses all content, in that the writer of such a work must have been the first amongst the literary men, just as Christ was the first amongst humanity. — If the deniers of the person of Jesus Christ do not believe such a thing, then they should draw up a different, just as divine, even if fabricated, image, and they will see that we are more righteous than they, in that we will not even deny our homage to the divine image drawn up by the poetic arts. — But if Christianity exists for as long as until this happens, then it is eternal, and the challengers of it will disperse like dust."

Reineck had already been waiting a long time to be able to speak a few words as well over this point, and continued, when Sigmann fell silent, in the following way, "What we heard yesterday and today amongst ourselves is of the sort that we can rejoice greatly over it; for the received and developed views are such irrevocable attributes of the truth of Christ that you must only regret those who strive to topple such a gigantic image. — They are in no position to describe a common nice everyday man, and yet have the audacity to outrageously impugn a divine image which is under all circumstances worthy of illuminating all of humanity. — I consider myself fortunate to have experienced yesterday and today where I have obtained through the wise views of our paternal teacher and finally through the utterances of my friends such conviction over the person and continuation of Christ amongst humanity in his divinely drawn up image as no cleverness and no event is capable of defeating anymore. — You fools! You blasphemers!, I now call out into the world. You want to destroy an image which reaches up into heaven and embraces humanity lovingly with its arms, meanwhile you are incapable of drawing a common man. — What are your gods of reason, your astronomic temples for our hearts? — Nothing but a hunt for ideas which heats up the brain and leaves the soul empty. — Therefore away with such antics which, instead of strengthening our life, weaken our life and give it nothing to hold on to. — Animate us, sublime image of our divine master, so that we will obtain in your light the human dignity, the Christian dignity which alone can lend us worth and assistance."

We were all enraptured by the rousing words of our friend and decided to close our discussion with it in order to finish the day in the mood in which we had been transported.

***

Fifteenth Lesson: The Miracles of Christ

When we assembled in the evening at Mr Rückmann's and had made him familiar with the results of our discussions the previous day, he expressed his unconcealed joy over the views we had come to, in that he said, "In whose inner-being the image of Christ, as the apostles drew it, has come to life, they have a guide through the winding paths of life who will lead them to the secure way out. — Indeed, anyone who feels this image within themselves is born again in spirit and need only watch over himself in order to bring this reborn one to maturity. — The creature and the worldly human indeed bristle against the spiritual product for as long as it is possible for them; only their power weakens from day to day until they finally succumb or die. — The one born in spirit can, however, not dispense with the characteristics which were previously so powerful, which as it were comprise the entire human, and he animates them with his powers, that is, awakes them from the dead. — Now the God-human has arisen and travels, after he has fortified himself appropriately, to heaven, and lives from now on entirely under the eternal influence of the primal power and of the divine word come to life in him. — The human lives in this state indeed also still in the here and now, but in heaven, to the extent heaven is within him. — Here we bump into a point of the teachings of Christ which, although extremely essential, is though seldom enough heeded. — Christ said, 'The kingdom of God cometh not with observation: Neither shall they say, Lo here! or, lo there! for, behold, the kingdom of God is within you'*.

As soon as we investigate these words appropriately, we must say that, if heaven is in the heart, then so too is the father, his angels, in a word, the entire power and glory of God in it. When we finally go further in these deductions,

---

*   [Tr.: Luke 17:20–21.]

then what was said here about heaven must also apply to hell, from which you can also not say, 'Lo here!' or 'Lo there!', but rather they must also be with all their powers and demons in the heart.

Considered from this point of view, the phenomena in the gospels obtain at once a different shape. — What previously were angels and devils are human characteristics; what is described as angels and devils are virtues and vices, good and evil urges and thoughts. — All objectivity is lifted up, and the human has only to look at himself in order to resolve all the miraculous phenomena of the gospels naturally.

If you endeavour to make these principles your own so that you will never be tempted anymore to seek good or evil spirits outside yourselves, then you will become perfect imitators of Christ, and his works, which are incomprehensible to both the orthodox supernaturalists and the limited rationalists, cannot be impenetrable to you for much longer. — In subjectivity is complete certainty; in objectivity, deception always reigns because spiritual powers are never to be perceived with outer senses, but only with inner senses. Since now this is irrevocably the case, we remain in all spiritual inquiries reliant on ourselves, and must, to the extent everything is contained in the human, obtain that knowledge by which we make ourselves competent, and which emanates from the purest light of omniscience. — The human is a mirror of God and all of nature. — Since we know now from experience that in a mirror, even if a small one, the objects are shown just as clearly as in a large one, the imperfection of human nature must not shock us here when it depicts a faithful mirror of everything which we see, or desire to know.

The so-called miracles of Christ separate into two classes. The first contains those which rest on external powers, on magnetic vibrations and impartations of special life powers. Anyone who knows the powers of life only to some extent knows then that throughout nature sucking in and radiating out, drawing in and pushing away dominate; anyone who can deny that from all herbs, fruits, and matter spiritual powers develop through fermentation, but the powers work through taste, smell, touch, and often through mere proximity; anyone who furthermore feels forced to admit to the attractive powers of magnets, the effects of galvanism, of electricity, of warmth and coldness must though necessarily attribute to the spirit which develops in a concentrated living structure still greater, finer, and more infallible powers. — In the life of the human a spirit develops which wants everything and can do anything and may only be sought in order to recognise all its characteristics and to learn to set them in operation.

From this class arise all of the conspicuous works of Christ which he performed on sick people. His awakened spirit, the radiance of his life, his firm will, and the purity of his body in the fullness of health had an electric effect on those sick people touched by his hand or breathed upon, so that it seemed as if the laws of nature had been overridden and a direct influence of God were present. — But when we consider the proposition that heaven with all its powers lies in the heart of the human, then such healings are extremely natural and it is only to be regretted that in our days such a power is counted under the rubric of supernatural miracles which are not believed and cannot be believed.

In the second class belong the works where Christ comes into contact with angels and spirits. — Here the sensory eye can see nothing anymore, but the spiritual can see everything. — When Christ drove out devils, then it is not a question according to the above principle of driving out a personified devil, but rather a characteristic firmly rooted in the human which his personality has completely mastered. — For the spiritual eye such characteristics vanish into demonic forms which, however, are only capable of being seen by those whose spirit has freed itself from all the bonds of the world and of hell. The human whom some vice has completely seized is no longer master of himself; the evil speaks from him often against his will; especially in the company of spiritual suitors, Satan shall rise up and resist in the body of a corrupted man in such a way that he is hardly to be endured anymore by the possessor, and the latter must either leave, or give vent with unseemly phrases. — I myself have learnt by experience that evil humans at such opportunities feel a seeming indisposition and must decide to have the demon driven out, or commence dealings with spiritually free people. — When the writers of the story of Christ portrayed such phenomena symbolically and personified, they did nothing but what the wisest before them and after them did and had to do just in order to give the matter at least some clarity. — To rebuke them over describing divine activity according to human behaviour is like reproaching that writer of fables, Aesop, for portraying the behaviour of humans amidst images of animals. — Where the explanation does not suffice anymore, the symbol must speak; but anyone who is too weak to explore a symbol should not behave like a boy who reproaches his custodian because he did not ask the moon to wait on the mountain until they had grabbed it by the horns.

There are yet phenomena in the Bible which belong to the first and second classes at the same time, and these are:

1) the birth of Christ;
2) the ascension to heaven; and
3) the feeding of the 4,000* and of the 5,000† people.

The birth of Christ belongs as symbol in the second class and points to the rebirth through the spirit. As natural event, however, we must count it in the first class in that it is connected in essence with the person of Christ. So enough of that. If we see each other again years from now, I promise to give you a complete explanation about it.

The ascension to heaven is, like the birth, symbolic and refers to the entrance to the kingdom of heaven in our hearts, but indicates at the same time that the vibrations of the spirit can overcome the weight of the body and bear it into the heights. — Here the rationalist screams oh and woe, and does not consider that you have had and still have this phenomenon in India since time immemorial, in that it belongs to the reputation of the penitents there who form the peculiar caste that from time to time one of them rises into the air by means of the power of the spirit and thereby justifies the meritoriousness of their procedure. An Englishman who saw such rising aloft could not comprehend the matter and thought an invisible cord fixed in a small tent had raised the man into the air, and made every endeavour to have such a cord produced.

---

*   [Tr.: Matthew 15:32–39 and Mark 8:1–10.]
†   [Tr.: Matthew 14:15–21, Mark 6:35–44, Luke 9:12–17, and John 6:5–15.]

But his expenditure and efforts were in vain, and he had to, for better or worse, believe in the soaring of the spirit.

Over the feeding of the 4,000 and of the 5,000 already some equivocal glosses have been made, and yet the moral intimation is so simple that any countryman understands it. Where the blessings of God reign, there is no lack — or, there the penny is turned into pounds. Symbolically this feeding points to the blessings of God. This feeding is therefore of the most beneficial influence for the devout in that it teaches that God will also bless the few, and those who trust in him are not left to go hungry. — In a real respect, however, this feeding and satiating is founded in the completely developed spiritual nature of the human in such a way that it is only called a miracle in so far as such development of the spirit is extremely rare, and thereby belongs under the unusual phenomena of world history. When you have once achieved practically what you now recognise theoretically, I will give you the most complete explanation of it. I do not consider myself authorised to speak about it before then. — All the other phenomena of the Bible, once they have resulted in becoming perfectly familiar to your spiritual powers, are explained by themselves, and will become as clear to you as seeing, hearing, and feeling. — The basis and the root of all knowledge, however, is the word which flows through the human and makes him familiar with the laws of nature and eternity. When you seek to obtain this with the means of assistance which we discussed, then you do not need mine, nor any other doctrine anymore; you feel yourself in the kingdom of the father free of all shackles and live the life in God which Christ predicted through his prophetic word for all his adherents and imitators."

Mr Rückmann fell silent. — I used the silence to direct a few words of thanks to him and at the same time add the request to give clearer information about the essentials of the divine word from which all power and knowledge seems to emanate. He seemed to think to himself and said, as before, the puzzling — "I must not."

Me: "What binds you? — A special promise or the nature of the matter?"

Him: "Both."

Me: "Is the former not to be broken?"

Him: "The former would bind me less, but the latter I cannot bypass."

Me: "Can nature want to have a secret?"

Him: "Not her, but humans."

Me: "The laws of nature are more important than those of humans."

Him: "Quite right, and hence I am bound."

Me: "Must you also not give an explanation of this?"

Him: "Oh yes."

Me: "So we ask about it, not only for our own sake, but rather for your goodness and generosity's sake so that we can never find reason to have to say you have set limits on your generosity."

Him: "You are right. In order to preserve your faith in me, I owe you an explanation. So listen.

No command can destroy the reflection of the light, just it pleases only in the change between day and night. — God is the holiest light. He wants to be considered holy. Only the feeling of sacredness which we harbour in his nearness can make us worthy of him. If human tongues wanted to explain systematically his nearness, then this nearness would directly destroy the feeling of holiness and make us unworthy of its possession. Hence silence on this point was made into a law and kept as one for as long as the world exists. — I cannot, as often as I have also already spoken against it, injure this law with pure conscience, and instead of a doctrine have only given intimations. — Follow the latter! — Exercise yourself in walking, standing, and speaking. — Inquire into the basis of creation according to the eternal spirit of creation so that your disposition and your way of thinking strengthen themselves in this generality and simplicity, and it will come to life in you; but then stamp the image of the sublime, divine founder of the Christian religion deep into your heart so that you have a secure light in all the unpleasant circumstances of life, and you will find that, when you succeed, you will, to penetrate into the kingdom of the father, to the primal law, see yet with delight and thankfulness this glorious paragon which has fulfilled everything that is to be fulfilled, and shown to humanity how high they can fly in the kingdoms of creation.

With these words I close the lessons given to you up to now without though refusing myself your visit. — I have on my boarding this ship taken on social commitments from which I freed myself for the sake of your company, but which I now must not leave unfulfilled any longer. — The ship's society gives evening conversations three times a week, for which I am obligated as a member. I have already often had to hear reproaches over my non-appearance. Only today I was admonished, and I gave my word to fulfill my promise in future in the case it was permitted for me to bring you, my friends, along into the company. The condition was naturally accepted straightaway, and so I invite you tomorrow evening to the party in the large cabin in order to be my guests there. You will get to know people of different classes and different education, which is not only useful for you, but necessary in order to not one day be surprised and embarrassed at any moment by different customs, gestures, manners, and ways of talking."

We did not know whether we should have rejoiced at this invitation or not, and made indecisive faces. Mr Rückmann noticed that and said, "I have given my word in your name and am convinced you will not compromise me." — We thanked him finally, gave our promise and left with a feeling of unease about the next evening that could not be hidden.

The next morning we came together a bit subdued on the deck. — It was as if the thought of that evening had put us all out of tune. One asked the other whether he had already ordered his suit and put himself in the state to be able to answer any questions appropriately. One laughed over such remarks, but without mastering one's awkwardness. — Grollmann said he thought the missionary institute had made no special contribution in selecting heroes like us to be missionaries. "We show timidity before a company of civilised, educated people in which we enter as invited guests — how will we feel at first when we want to enter a town or a village where they dispute not only our right to speak, but our entry?" — "Towards them," replied Bentheim, "we will hold up the image of our crucified saviour and call to them that we are bringing them a salvation from death." — "And if they answer us with stones?", responded Reineck. — "Then we have done our part," he excused himself. —

I finally entered this debate and said, "My friends! It seems to me that we are behaving like children who are scared of a phantom. The company in which we will enter consists of educated people who will accept us as we are, not as we should be according to their ideas and expectations. We will also not find everything in such a way that we cannot wish for something more. — Mr Rückmann has made an effort to prepare us for all the coming circumstances of life, and his lessons must have had little effect in us if we do not know how to act properly in a social order. The company in which we are invited shall serve us as a means for practising what we have learnt and for learning to approach people in a friendly way. In this respect, we are doubly indebted to Mr Rückmann who has created us this opportunity. I for my person will therefore perform my usual business until the time when I go to the party and not think of it again until I find myself there."

Everybody applauded me and promised to do the same.

***

An Outline of the Life of Johann Baptist Krebs

*(translated from an obituary written in 1851
for his Freemasons' lodge in Stuttgart —
Wilhelm zur aufgehenden Sonne)*

When we take a look at the completed earthly life of a man, and see how throughout a long career he always spent his powers on noble goals, how he was almost always accompanied by fortune, rewarded with acclaim, and favoured by health and physical strength, then we feel through this a satisfaction which is related only to that which the harmony of beauty awakes. With every right, this is to be applied to the honourable man to whose memory these lines are dedicated, to **Johann Baptist Krebs**, whose meritorious life ended in Stuttgart. on 2nd October 1851 in his 77th year. He was born on 12th April 1774 in the grand-ducal Baden village Überauchen in Villingen. His parents were penniless country people. —

Thus arisen from the happy seclusion of country life, the rare fortune was granted him, which the poet celebrates so beautifully, of being permitted to spend the years of his childhood with open mind for all beauty "far from life-confusing circles"[*] in the unspoilt harmless quiet of rustic farmland.

When talent and inclination led the youth to the scientific profession, and indeed to that which led to the investigation of divine matters before others, and took his path at first to the heights of human knowledge in order to dare from these a timid look into the depths of divine wisdom, there too the happiness was granted to him which was yearned for in vain and envied by thousands, the satisfaction of the most noble of desires, the thirst for knowing, from the sources of science.

---

[*]   [Tr.: from Friedrich von Schiller's *Die Braut von Messina* [The Bride of Messina] IV, 7.]

After he had received the necessary preparatory training at the high school of Villingen and Constance, he went to Freiburg im Breisgau where he studied Catholic theology for two years with much zeal. But his amiable aptitude led him from the serious lecture halls of science to a more attractive goal, to the cheerful art.

From Freiberg im Breisgau he often went to Donaueschingen, and there he made the acquaintance of several significant members of the royal court orchestra, and especially that of the singer Weiß who also enjoyed an honourable renown as a singing teacher. Since Krebs had opportunity there to hear the barely first appearing masterworks of Mozart, Haydn, and other eminences of the art in the highest possible perfection, he was himself also encouraged to recite at apt opportunities various vocal compositions, which found general approval, so more and more the wish and the resolve was stirred in him to dedicate himself exclusively to the art, all the more since the royal court singer Weiß became aware of a musical talent of a rare sort in our late friend in addition to his beautifully metal-rich voice and became his teacher and guide, and first introduced him into the inner sacred halls of the divine art. In the year 1795 Krebs travelled, prepared by an excellent school and provided with favourable recommendations, to Stuttgart where he immediately received a position as court singer which he never left again. The rare natural gift with which the creator had outfitted him unfolded now more and more into acknowledged mastery. Through untiring, eager study, he arrived at knowledge of the greatest masterworks, and at a comprehensive magnificent view of music overall. Productive for his development were also several artistic journeys which he made to Munich, Vienna, Berlin, and Weimar; everywhere he was accorded the friendliest reception, and many an acquaintanceship which was of influence on his entire life was connected with this origin.

Amongst the various genres of musical compositions, it was not only the dramatic though in which Krebs shone just as much through his rare talent, as through the truth, the emotion of his recital. His soul, filled by the infinite greatness of the divinity, drew him also mightily towards church music, and many still live who recall with joy his lifting song which sounded like a voice of heaven out of the invisible. Especially when his melodious voice resounded in the hymn, that most profound foundation of sacred music, and that song of praise natural to man in which a soul full of feeling comes to speak, the audience could not escape the impression of enormous superiority of the creator in the creation.

Up until the end of his life, music, song, and poetry still provided him with great pleasure. When he had withdrawn his artistic activity entirely from the public stage, the untiringly active man filled his free hours with philosophical and aesthetic studies, composed a number of beloved arias, duets, songs, and oratorios, and still held for twenty years, next to his service as opera director, formally the office of an opera writer.

Often he could say, 'Music attracts me also because amidst all the arts and sciences almost none are so sharply bounded and enclosed as it. To its seven tones, no more are to be added, and yet it is in its productions infinite. As long as passions are in the human breast, as long as every emotion speaks in tones, again and again will new favourite melodies resound with the seven ancient tones.'

His artistic achievements also received the most abundant recognition, and if enthusiastic storms of applause, if signs of thanks of all sorts for enthralling, truly lifting enjoyment of quickly vanishing hours contribute to the life's happiness of a human, then he is to be counted as one of the happiest.

Even when his spirit had turned entirely to the eternal, to the supernatural, music still exercised an essential influence on the path of development which he followed. Like in the school of Pythagoras, for him music and geometry were also mighty means of awakening of the spiritual life, and just as in music the chords gave him the laws of harmony, so too in geometry he sought the laws for harmony in architecture, in particular in the Gothic for which he had a great interest. He believed he had found in the human body itself the scale in which we can climb up and down and by which our inner ear is sharpened for the perception of the inner voice, indeed all of nature revealed to him by means of a rule embracing the universe an audible world order. Thus Krebs was a high priest of music in that high encompassing sense of the word in which Plato used it, and according to which music comprehends in itself as art of the muses in general the sciences and the arts, indeed even philosophy as the highest music, leading as the highest and most perfect human development to the purest nobility of soul, to free conformity to law.

Hence neither artistic fame, nor the acclaim of contemporaries, were the only and most principal adornment of his life, were the only and most principal source of his happiness. Artistic creations of every sort indeed contribute no less to adornment, to the beautification and amusement of earthly life; but there is yet another, yet a more certain source of true earthly happiness, it is wisdom which the structure of an earthly life must lead to if its happiness should rest on more certain foundations, and which was unshakeably the goal which he had before his eyes.

Krebs belonged to the inquiring spirits in whose soul the need for knowing cannot fall silent, whose soul fulfils the desire, of the countless problems which nature places before us at every moment, to solve those which are most important for our salvation. His striving spirit strained all the powers of his soul to work through the difficulties of the investigation, in the hope of finding the full light on the other side of these obscurities. — He repeatedly read through the books of sacred scripture, only his understanding of them was not yet realised, and his free spirit bristled against having his thoughts shackled to a belief system. He studied the philosophical systems of antiquity and of modern times, but found only the history of aberrations of the human spirit, the unpleasant result of the transience of everything earthly, even the for a long time highly praised edifice of philosophical acumen. He saw the most profound thinkers on the bounds of experience, in eternal wars over the properties of the hereafter, without even a foot of that unknown land being obtained with all these wars. But he did not allow himself to be discouraged; his stimulated power of thought strived out into the infinite, he wanted insight, truth, and became all the more eager for this truth, the more difficult and more concealed it seemed to him. He no longer wanted to expend his powers uselessly on the path trodden up to then; a new way was revealed to him in Freemasonry, which he hoped to lead him to the goal.

A new light went on in him, a voice from the innermost being of his heart was heard, and it called to him, 'You have abandoned your own house, and seek ease in foreign parts; you have flown from the source, and seek refreshment in the wastes. Return! Recognise yourself!' To complete this task, to fathom the deep sense of the Masonic symbols now remained unshakeably the aim of his striving for thirty years, and to whom of us should it be unknown what he achieved in this area, how he was one of the most enlightened Masons of his time, and was in particular the living soul of our lodge?

An activity of this sort could not fail to yet beautify the evening of his life when he had retired after a very eventful life as an artist. — Bearing the spirit of religious inquiry within himself, it could not remain enclosed in the innermost seat of his disposition, but had to, like every feeling, seek to obtain an outer form. Penetrating the powers of his soul, and the entire extent of his life, it was portrayed in his oral and written lectures, just as in his fiction. Enthused for his ideas, he went in the direction which he was following completely without fear or doubt, and he worked until the end of his life for its dissemination, untiring, whether he received acclaim or not, carried by his inner power, through the consciousness of the truth of his matter and of his honest will.

He appeared like an envoy of God in an age where scepticism had almost become general amongst the educated classes. With the bold courage of a prophet, although himself broad-minded and a free thinker in the noblest and most beautiful sense of the word, he stood up to that reigning spirit of tepid indifference. With the force of a prophet he drew the blindfold from the eyes of the blindfolded, and sharpened their eyes for a more worthy, more meaningful, more stimulating way of looking at the sacred documents of religion. With the enthusiasm of a prophet he made accessible to those afflicted with blindness and wandering around in foolishness and ignorance the outlines of that venerable poetry. With the eager love, though purified by the mildness of his character, of a prophet, he led the brothers on the path of genuine, illuminated, inquiring thought. With the oratorical power of a prophet he drew the brothers of that class and age into our temple to listen to his words.

What was the secret of the power of attraction which he exercised on us all? Was it not his fraternal love which he so often, almost in every one of his descriptions, announced with ardent zeal, which he bore stamped on himself in the amiability of his countenance, which he strove to prove in the word? Was it not his natural, unfeigned, hearty benevolence which even because of that was recognised perhaps more deeply and valued perhaps more highly by the child-like minds of the sisters than by the brothers themselves, and which is now also felt deeply and regretted painfully after it has stopped being present instructively and beneficially to them in its outward guise, because the beauty and high value of the noble, disinterested love can only be properly treasured and valued by the disposition, not by the mind.

In his old age, when Krebs had turned entirely to the supernatural, he resembled those natures, only known to us from tradition and arising purely from the hand of the creator, to whom God reveals himself and whose life is a sublime conversation with God. His modesty, however, never let the thought arise in him that he really belonged to the favoured beings whom nature gifted with preeminent gifts of recognising the supernatural. His love of humanity wanted to give the peace he had found to others too; hence an invisible force drove him to make his discovery a common good; hence his striving went its way to return the royal art to firm practical principles. — Directly for that reason, because it is designated for the use and benefit of all, he claimed it must also be accessible to all, and enlighten all those who dedicate themselves to it; everybody must be able to demonstrate the correctness of its doctrine to themselves.

This was for him irrevocable truth which he pronounced with the full power of conviction constantly from the altar, in everyday conversation, and in his writings.

It cannot be the task of this depiction to give an if only condensed overview of his many writings appearing under the name of Kerning or even an assessment of them. Only so much must not be unmentioned, that these writings, particularly his Freemasonry writings and his *Missionaries* caused a great sensation in the Masonic world, and even led to him brothers from distant lands who wanted to get to know the author personally.

No other writer either has expressed the concept of Masonry as a specific thing as sharply and placed it at the top and carried it out with such a creative spirit as he did. Hence the rigorous construction, the precise coherence of the content of his writings. They are all as if from *one* mould; like a thread the leading ideas draw through everything amidst the most various forms. With that Krebs possessed the gift of making himself clear by examples, although, already on account of the newness of the subject which is too foreign to the common sphere of thought, he could not avoid remaining obscure about a lot.

Hence he also could not possibly, notwithstanding the manifold acknowledgement which his writings found, escape all attacks. He was reproached from various sides with mysticism, and this reproach, tossed off so easily without any foundation, will be justified if we examine him somewhat more closely.

What should he then actually express? — All those who described processes of their inner life which have mostly not taken place in the life of most humans, or remained unheeded, have been named mystics since time immemorial, and such descriptions will also receive this lot in future because by far most humans are lacking in their requisite own experience. For others by comparison, whose life has already experienced those changes, such descriptions can perhaps be quite clear and understandable.

So the writings of our master will certainly also find their approbation with those who are more advanced in the area of inner experiences.

However that might also be, how it may stand with the doctrine pronounced by him — it emerged in any case from his tireless striving for truth. He also had *the* truth which was achievable for him, not *the* truth which resides only with the omniscient, for no mortal eye can grasp its brilliance, its weak shimmer only illuminates sparingly our steps into the regions of darkness. Now he has entered into the master's realm and will see solved the puzzle which could still unsettle him here.

After we have now thrown a glance at the long career of the immortalised one, we will attempt to recall the image of the whole man. The wistful feeling which must be awakened at his loss will find its alleviation in the contemplation of such a worthy personage preserved by a long, happy, and honourable life. Krebs belonged to those men whose outer-being already fascinated and led to the expectation of an unusual nature. He was of medium height, more tall than small, his body was well-formed and strongly built. His countenance was large, with winning masculine features which expressed yet more mildness than earnestness; his beautiful blue eyes, covered more than usual by the eyelids on the outer sides, his animated, penetrating gaze, his wavy hair, all announced the inner fire of his spirit and his disposition; his erect posture showed the straight, decisive part of his character. He was one of those normal, powerful natures which his homeland, the upper Black Forest, not uncommonly produced, ennobled by the art of vivid portrayal. His spiritual being was in harmony with the physical. I do not want to offend the law of truth in that I attribute to him a few of those mighty, preeminent powers which call forth great changes in art and science; it is not necessary to add anything to his works in order to gain recognition for his name with his fellow men and the future world.

In the Masonic world he will also in the future stand there as an inviolable great. With the brothers of our lodge, however, what will never vanish from memory is with what abundance of spirit, how mildly and strongly, and how stirringly and encouragingly he spoke from the altar.

Every one of us contributes to the building of the temple on which we work a building block, and were it even so small; but he, the high master, was a granite pillar of this temple. The breath which animated his soul, the fundamental idea which he pronounced, penetrated through all his writings, and so long as these are read by his Masonic brothers, his name will also not perish.

In his circle of friends his spirit liked to move in all the directions of knowledge, and when he lingered alone in the green shade of his garden, and had directed his inner gaze on the depths of Freemasonry which were accessible to him, how his venerable head brightened up then, how his features rejuvenated themselves! His spirit and body, powerful until the end, absolutely delivered a spoken evidence that genuine enthusiasm also opens an entirely new source of life for the body, and pours an abundance of powers over it. Certainly it must be a higher, spiritual striving in which the disposition also takes part with the entire strength of its noblest interests, and we can only thank the great architect of the world that he led him by the angel of peace into the eternal east before a decay of his powers had to appear according to an implacable law of nature.

From this outline of his life put together in narrow bounds, we see that our late master united in himself various talents and powers which already give grounds for individual fame and distinction. Whereas the youth and young man offered us through his rare talent the purest greetings of art, the old man made accessible to us in meaningful hieroglyphic writing the puzzle of existence, and these various powers met in him in such rich abundance, in such high power and such perfect harmony, in such wonderful interplay and such prominent originality, in such inexhaustible fruitfulness as has only ever been the case with a few especially favoured men.

When we think now that all that was bound up in him with the warmest, most purified religiosity, with the most untainted purity of morals, with the most magnanimous zeal for human welfare, with the tenderest, most devoted receptivity for love and friendship, then we may well claim that in him the purely human emerged in the most abundant perfection and transfiguration.

Let us now yet recall the last moments in the life of our master.

It was on 15th September when he was struck on a walk by a violent attack of dizziness which forced him to immediately return. He did not reach his quiet chamber without injury anymore, for in the vicinity of his house this dizziness overcame him so much that he fell and wounded himself on the forehead over the right eye. The blood streamed from this wound. The doctor, who had been called quickly, straightaway declared this loss of blood to be fortunate, and nobody suspected danger. Next to the relations of our beloved brother, the brothers from the Orient hurried over to loyally wait on and tend to him in order to prove to the dear master of all what ardent love is capable of. The patient now seemingly neared the desired improvement daily, and like in previous times he was soon again the heart-warming and happy childlike nature. With bold hope the brothers dreamed already of the master at the altar; they saw him already standing again in the chains, and one eye announced to the other joyfully the message: 'it is going well!'. But after fourteen days a change occurred quickly and unexpectedly. To the present suffering was added a catarrhal fever, and the patient quite soon felt that — if this fever were not overcome in a short time — the final hour was not distant for him anymore. He shared this with those present with as much indisputable certainty as the just as firm courage with which he looked death in the eye.

Although the brothers attending him *could* not believe the dry words of approaching death, did not *want* to believe them, they were though convinced by the growing worsening of the dangerous state of the dear master, and with indescribable sadness they recognised the quickly approaching misfortune.

On the second day of this month the fever had reached its highpoint, but the all too weakened body was incapable of claiming mastery, and blessed with full consciousness, the ardently beloved passed away at midday as gently and peacefully as if he were lying down to the accustomed rest. The sad news was sent to all parts, and as if on the wings of a storm the shocking words disseminated themselves in the circles of brothers: 'the master is dead!' It was *one* cry of pain, *one* call of woe which penetrated through the chain of brothers. The ring of the noblest and most beautiful had indeed been shattered quickly and unexpectedly:

> From us the father takes his leave,
> The dear man taken by cold death;
> The master dead! Oh let us weep,
> Our tears shall alleviate our bitter grief.

The solemn funeral of the beloved deceased was set for the eleventh hour of the first Sunday in October. From near and far the brothers appeared early in order to once more look on the highly esteemed master, the dear teacher, and to offer him their hand for the last time.

The death knell echoed dully through the busy city; already the coffin had been blessed and consecrated, and mournful sounds announced the beginning of a ceremony for which young and old, high and low had gathered. The funeral procession was led by the circles to whom the deceased had belonged in life; the lodge whose master of the chair he was, and that of the three cedars* — they formed the column to which a great number of admirers of the deceased joined themselves. In all the streets through which the procession moved, an immeasurable crowd of people had positioned itself; the participation in this sad event was so general and so hearty that Stuttgart's walls had probably not seen a similar funeral procession for many years.

Sounds of mourning received the coffin at the cemetery — brothers carried it to the grave which was already surrounded by a row of sisters before the arrival. They wanted to show their infinitely beloved teacher the last honour.

Amidst the singing of the choir of the royal court theatre, accompanied by the royal court orchestra, the coffin was entrusted to the earth, and now the city pastor Dannecker spoke a short sermon after he had consecrated the last resting place of the deceased.

After the end of this sermon, an elevating song by the members of the opera and the choir followed, after which Brother Löwe recited a moving poem.

Again a charming song sounded; during which Brother Walbach spoke a few words of farewell, after which a song of mourning by the singing circle whose honourable member the deceased had been for many years concluded the august ceremony.

Hot tears ran into the grave, and with bleeding hearts the brothers parted from the unforgettable one. One consoled the other with the words: 'He is still among us!'

And may these words now always also remain true!

---

*   [Tr.: the Freemasons' lodge 'Zu den 3 Cedern'.]

The love and veneration which all the brothers bestowed on him hallows and consecrates also from now on for the earth and the heaven in them the pure, true fraternal love. It pours itself in all directions over all the members of the lodge as a benedictive legacy of the master, lends them strength and unity to continue his work, and forms a firm central point in which they will all come together always.

And so now rest from your restless activity, you brave fighter for truth and your conviction! The well-earned laurels, they have indeed not adorned your brow, but it gleams with ample evergreen leaves in the unwilting love of your brothers. No monument by an artist's hand adorns your grave mound either, but a more beautiful one is erected for you by every heart in which you awake the heavenly spark of love.

***

**Other works by Johann Baptist Krebs
published by K A Nitz**

Paths to Immortality
Based on the Undeniable Powers
of Human Nature

Christianity
or
God and Nature Only One
Through the Word